Field Guide to Grasses of the Mid-Atlantic

A KEYSTONE BOOK

Keystone Books are intended to serve the citizens
of Pennsylvania. They are accessible, well-researched
explorations into the history, culture, society, and
environment of the Keystone State as part of the Middle
Atlantic region.

Field Guide

to Grasses

of the

Mid–Atlantic

Sarah Chamberlain

The Pennsylvania
State University Press
University Park,
Pennsylvania

Library of Congress Cataloging-in-Publication Data

Names: Chamberlain, Sarah, 1964– author.
Title: Field guide to grasses of the mid-atlantic / Sarah
    Chamberlain.
Description: University Park, Pennsylvania : The
    Pennsylvania State University Press, [2018] | "Keystone
    books." | Includes bibliographical references and index.
Summary: "A guide, geared toward all levels of botanical
    knowledge, to identifying over 300 species of grasses
    found in four physiographic provinces within the Mid-
    Atlantic Region"—Provided by publisher.
Identifiers: LCCN 2017024346 | ISBN 9780271078694 (cloth
    : alk. paper)
Subjects: LCSH: Grasses—Middle Atlantic States—
    Identification.
Classification: LCC QK495.G74 C464 2018 | DDC 584/.9—
    dc23
LC record available at https://lccn.loc.gov/2017024346

Published by The Pennsylvania State University Press,
University Park, PA 16802-1003

Second printing, 2019

The Pennsylvania State University Press is a member of the
Association of University Presses.

It is the policy of The Pennsylvania State University Press to
use acid-free paper. Publications on uncoated stock satisfy
the minimum requirements of American National Standard
for Information Sciences—Permanence of Paper for Printed
Library Material, ANSI z39.48-1992.

To Ken Dunne,

mentor,

friend, and

fellow

grass nerd.

I have just made out my first Grass, hurrah!

hurrah! I must confess that Fortune favours the

bold, for as good luck would have it, it was the

easy Anthoxanthum odoratum: nevertheless it is

a great discovery; I never expected to make out

a grass in all my life. So Hurrah. It has done my

stomach surprising good.

—Letter from Charles Darwin to J. D. Hooker,

June 5, [1855]

Contents

Preface

Grasses are one of the most ubiquitous plant groups on earth. The grass family (Poaceae) contains more species than almost every other flowering plant family, surpassed only by the orchids, asters, and legumes. Grasses inhabit a wide geographic range, from the tropical to the boreal, and are found in both wet and dry habitats. They dominate the tall grass prairies of the Midwest, the Great Plains, the oak savannas of the west and southwest, and the salt marshes along our coasts. They are an integral component of the flora of many other open habitats as well, including fields, freshwater marshes, and our beloved suburban lawns. Grasses, in the form of grains, are also a staple in the diets of many cultures. Wheat, barley, rye, oats, sorghum, corn, rice, and other cereal grasses are either consumed directly or used as ingredients in many foods. Indeed, it is hard to imagine a modern diet that does not include some kind of grain. Grasses are also used as thatching (*Phragmites australis*), burned in Native American ceremonies (*Anthoxanthum nitens*), and woven with other plants to make baskets (*Muhlenbergia filipes*).

Although grasses are common in many habitats, as a group, they are typically difficult to identify. The minute parts of the grass flower, along with unfamiliar and specialized terminology, make grasses challenging to most who attempt identification. In the mid-Atlantic region, existing grass taxonomies and field manuals are either too vague to assist in identifying all but the most common grasses or too technical for even a seasoned botanist to comprehend. My goal in writing this guide was to provide an easily accessible treatment of grasses geared toward all levels of botanical knowledge and experience. The characters used to identify the different genera and species are ones that, for the most part, are easily observed and understood. I truly believe that if presented in the right context, grasses can be mastered by anyone willing to put forth the effort to learn about this unique and beautiful group of plants.

This field guide encompasses the mid-Atlantic region, including eight states either wholly or in part (map 1). More than three hundred grasses found within the region are included in this guide. They occupy a constellation of habitats and include the very common smooth brome (*Bromus inermis*) to the uncommon wood millet (*Milium effusum*). In creating this list, I did not include waifs, garden escapes, or cultivated grasses, unless

Map 1. Area covered by this field guide. The shaded area corresponds to the following J. M. Omernik Level III Ecoregions (1987) either wholly or in part: Blue Ridge Mountains, Erie/Ontario Lake Hills and Plain, Central Appalachian, Central Appalachian Ridge and Valleys, Middle Atlantic Coastal Plain, North Central Appalachians, Northern Appalachian Plateau and Uplands, Northern Piedmont, Piedmont, Southeastern Plains, and Western Allegheny Plateau.

they have become naturalized. I also did not consider varieties or subspecies, unless I felt there was a compelling reason to do so.

The guide is organized as a dichotomous key (although in some instances there are more than two choices). The first part of the key includes all the grass genera as well as monospecific taxa—that is, genera with only a single species. The second part of the key is for those genera with more than one species. In organizing the key, I tried to position all of the unusual grasses first, so that if users become familiar with these taxa, they will be able to easily maneuver through this section.

In the introductory section, titled "How to Use This Guide," I also present three unusual grasses: ones with a rame spikelet arrangement, the Phalaridae tribe, and the Paniceae tribe. I urge users to study these grasses. Mastering these taxa will result in a much easier time with identification. I have included a number of pages on the parts of the grass with salient information that will help with identification. I also included a section on dense spikelike panicles. These grasses are often hard to identify because the inflorescence branches are tightly compact and the spikelets are often obscured by bristles, awns, or hairs. Most of the grasses covered in this section of the book are also covered elsewhere in the guide so that the user has more than one opportunity to arrive at the correct identification.

Nomenclature generally (but not always) follows the Flora of North America. Synonyms are given for some taxa and are included in brackets after the accepted name. For habitat descriptions, I relied heavily on Gleason and Cronquist 1991 and Weakley 2015. Keys to the species are based on these sources, as well as the keys of Rhoads and Block 2007, with additional information gleaned from specimens housed at the PAC Herbarium at Penn State University and GrassBase, an online database (Clayton et al. 2006–). Plant distribution maps (by physiographic province) are based on information available from online plant atlases for Delaware, Maryland, New York, Pennsylvania, Virginia, and West Virginia. Information for Ohio and New Jersey are from the United States Department of Agriculture (USDA) PLANTS database, with additional assistance from Kathleen Walz, New Jersey Natural Heritage Program Ecologist, New Jersey Department of Environmental Protection; Linda Kelly, independent contractor; and David Snyder, State Botanist, Natural Heritage Program in New Jersey. Maps for monotypic species in the region are included in the General Key, while those with two or more species are found in the Genera Keys. Users are urged to consult the Utah State University's *Flora of North America* website (2008) and GrassBase (Clayton et al. 2006–) for more information on the grasses covered here, including distribution maps, additional descriptors, and line drawings.

Wetland Indicator Status is from the United States Army Corps of Engineers' (USACE) 2014 National Wetland Plant List, version 3.2 (since updated to 3.3) and is abbreviated as follows:

Obligate (OBL)	almost always occur in wetlands
Facultative wetland (FACW)	usually occur in wetlands, but may occur in nonwetlands
Facultative (FAC)	occur in wetlands and nonwetlands
Facultative upland (FACU)	usually occur in nonwetlands, but may occur in wetlands
Upland (UPL)	almost always occur in uplands

The status is given for the Atlantic and Gulf Coast Plain and the Eastern Mountains and Piedmont. If both regions have the same status, a single status is given. Unless otherwise noted, illustrations are from the Hunt Botanical Institute's Hitchcock-Chase Collection of Grass Drawings (2016).

Acknowledgments

I would like to thank the Department of Geography at The Pennsylvania State University and Riparia—a research center within the department—and its director, Dr. Robert Brooks, for providing financial support for this project. The Pennsylvania Native Plant Society and Riparia provided funds to complete some crucial drawings for this guide and their support is invaluable to the success of the project. I would also like to thank the following organizations and individuals for their financial support of this publication: the Pennsylvania Department of Environmental Protection; RETTEW Associates, Inc.; the Virginia Native Plant Society, Potowmack Chapter Grass Bunch; the West Virginia Native Plant Society; The WHM Group; Susan Berry; Matt Bright; Joseph Chamberlain Sr. and Ellen Chamberlain; Joseph Chamberlain Jr. and Ellen Chamberlain; Margaret Chatham; Margaret Fisher; Alan M. Ford; Clifton Gay; Ruth Gibbons; Carolyn Haynes; James Irre; Catherine Ledec; Elizabeth Martin; James McGlone and Deana Crumbling; Gale Minnich-Blewis; Karen Monroe; Rhonda Ridley; Beverley Rivera; Barbara Ryan; Charles Smith; Susan Turnbach; Denice H. Wardrop; and Mary K. Wharton. Kathryn Yahner and the staff at Penn State University Press were integral to ensuring a smooth path to publication, and I appreciate their resourcefulness and guidance. I am grateful as well for the assistance I received from the staff and interns at Riparia. Hannah Ingram dedicated many long hours to refining line drawings and creating maps. She is both a valued colleague and a friend. Dylan Kubina, Adam Larson, Nicole Hain, and Spencer Haley helped with various aspects of the guide, including testing keys, researching wetland status information, and creating the glossary and maps. Lugene Bruno at the Hunt Institute handled my many urgent requests for line drawings with extraordinary speed, patience, and aplomb. This book would not have been possible without her assistance. Ann Passmore and her staff at the Pattee Library's Digitization and Preservation Center dedicated many hours to imaging line drawings, and their assistance is gratefully recognized. Elizabeth Farnsworth, Senior Research Ecologist for the New England Wildflower

Society, gave me permission to use some of her existing grass drawings and created some of the drawings for this book. I thank her for her generosity and artistic pen. Loree Speedy and Mark Bowers, as well as the many students who participated in my workshops over the years, field tested earlier versions of the guide and provided several helpful comments. Finally, thanks to my family and friends, whose support made this guide possible. To my parents, Ellen and Joe, many thanks for your steadfast support and love. To my children, Jake and Andy, I appreciate your patience during the many long days and nights that I worked on this book. You are my everything! And in answer to your perennial question: Yes, my guide is finally done.

How to Use This Guide

The *Field Guide to Grasses of the Mid-Atlantic* is organized in the form of a dichotomous key. The reader is given a "couplet" comprising two (or more) descriptive phrases. The reader selects the phrase that best describes the grass specimen in question and then follows that branch in the key. These steps are repeated until the grass has been identified.

The guide comprises two keys: (1) a genus key, beginning on page 18, that includes all genera as well as monospecific grasses (genera with only a single species) and (2) genera keys (for genera with two or more species) that starts on page 78. If the genus is already known, readers may choose to go directly to the appropriate species key.

Readers should review these guidelines and become familiar with some of the more unusual grasses on pages 13–15 before attempting to use the guide. Also, a ten-power (10×) hand lens is recommended for field identification. Some grasses, however, will require greater magnification and must be collected and keyed using a dissecting microscope.

General Suggestions

1. The keys in this guide rely primarily on grass flowers (inflorescence type, spikelet and floret characterisitcs). However, there are some grasses that can be identified solely using vegetative characters. These include Japanese stiltgrass (*Microstegium vimineum*) and bristle basketgrass (*Oplismenus hirtellus*) [distinctive leaves] and velvet grass (*Holcus*) [velvety sheaths]. Learning these species and their distinctive vegetative characters will aid in identification.

2. The key will be easier to use if you select a mature grass specimen (after it blooms and goes to seed). If you dissect the floret and see stamens and feathery stigma, you're too early.

3. Make sure you look at more than one spikelet, lemma, leaf, and so on before coming to a conclusion.
4. Read all the choices before making a decision (and note that sometimes there are more than two choices).
5. Use the drawings, tips, and notes to help guide your decision; they provide important information for keying.
6. Use both *habitat* (coastal, inland, etc.) and *habit* (the growth form of the plant) to help in your identification.
7. Resist the urge to *top snatch* (grabbing only the aboveground portion of the plant) when collecting a specimen. Many grasses require you to examine the belowground structures to make a positive identification.
8. *DO NOT collect any grasses you suspect may have special status (rare, threatened, or endangered)! Take notes and/or photographs instead.*

Deciphering a Grass Entry

Symbols

±	more or less
>	greater than
≥	greater than or equal to
<	less than
≤	less than or equal to
†	non-native
♂	male
♀	female

scientific name (in italics) — *Agrostis capillaris*† (Rhode Island bent). indicates grass is not native to the mid-Atlantic region — common name (in parentheses). Meadows, roadsides, disturbed areas; FAC. wetland indicator status — typical habitat(s) where grass occurs

Glossary

annual completing growth (flowering and fruiting) within one year, the plant then dying

appressed a plant part that is closely associated with another part, as in "leaves appressed to the stem"

ascending pointing in an upward direction

auricle ear-shaped extension from one or both sides of the base of the foliage leaf blade/apex of the foliage leaf sheath

awn bristlelike extension of the nerve of a lemma or glume

axillary borne in the axil of the leaf or stem

bearded callus short hairs present at the base of the floret (callus)

bifid divided by a deep cleft or notch into two parts; forked

bisexual both sexes are present, e.g., a flower with both male (stamens) and female (pistils) parts

blade broad part of a leaf apart from the petiole

bract modified leaf or scale, with a flower cluster in its axil; sometimes larger than the true flower

callus	hard, commonly pointed base of the floret or the spikelet, just above the point of disarticulation
ciliate	having a fringe of hairs
coiled	shaped as a spiral or series of loops
collar	base of the leaf blade where it meets the sheath
compressed	flattened
culm	grass stem
decumbent	lying along the ground or along a surface, with upward curving tips
dense spikelike panicle	superficially resembles a spike, but is actually a panicle because the inflorescence branches more than once; branching is often difficult to see
digitate cluster	inflorescence where all branches originate from the same point (or approximately the same point), like the fingers (digits) on a hand
disarticulate	separate, as when spikelets or florets separate from the rachis of the inflorescence when the grass is mature; disarticulation can occur above or below the glumes
ellipsoid	in the shape of an ellipse
erect	rigidly upright or straight
fertile	able to produce seed
floret	grass flower consisting of the pistil and the stamens, which are enclosed by two scales (bracts), the lemma and the palea
glaucous	having a whitish or bluish cast
glume	membranous bract surrounding the floret of grass, usually present in pairs as a lower (first) and upper (second) glume; the glumes plus the floret equals the spikelet
inflorescence	flower-bearing portion of the grass; the most common inflorescences in grasses are spikes, racemes, and panicles
intermediate	positioned between two other structures, as in the intermediate vein of the lemma
keel (keeled)	ridge that forms when a structure like a palea, lemma, or leaf sheath is folded lengthwise; commonly a vein is present along its length
lemma	lower of the two bracts that enclose the grass flower
ligule	membranous scale, sometimes reduced to a ring of hairs, on the inner side of the leaf sheath at its junction with the blade
lucid	clear or transparent
margin	border of a leaf, lemma, or other structure
membranaceous	thin, membranelike in texture; papery
minute	tiny
nerve	manifestation of the vascular tissue in a grass leaf or spikelet; may be impressed or raised (see also vein)
node	point on the stem where the leaf is inserted; joint
open panicle	panicle in which the branches are widely spreading, diffuse
palea	upper of the two bracts that enclose the grass flower
panicle	elongate, branched inflorescence with pedicellate spikelets (main panicle branches are divided into smaller branchlets)
pedicel	stalk of the inflorescence or spikelet; in grasses, synonymous with the peduncle
pedicellate	stalked, with a pedicel
peduncle	stalk of a flower or fruit

perennial	growing and surviving over several or many years; perennials generally flower and fruit annually
pistil	seed-bearing organ of the flower, made up of the ovary, stigma, and style
pustulose	having little blisters or pustules
raceme	elongate, unbranched inflorescence with pedicellate spikelets
rachilla	pedicel of the individual floret within the spikelet; the rachilla may be remnant in spikelets with a single floret
rachilla prolonged behind the palea	situation in which the rachilla of the upper floret remains attached to the floret below it; since the rachilla attaches on the inner (palea) side of the floret, the rachilla is thus "prolonged behind the palea"
rachis	portion of the stem within the inflorescence
rame	inflorescence where the spikelets are paired at each node, the first sessile, the other pedicellate
reflexed	turned abruptly backward
rhizome	whitish belowground horizontal stem
scabrous	rough to the touch because of the epidermis or the presence of short, stiff hairs
scarious	membranous, dry, and brownish in color
secund	spikelets all on one side of the rachis (often by twisting of pedicels)
sessile	lacking a pedicel or stalk
sheath	lower part of the leaf that encircles the stem; the margin is free and overlapping in most grasses, but in a few cases the margins are fused, forming a tube
spathe	large bract underlying and often enclosing an inflorescence
spike	unbranched inflorescence where the sessile spikelets sit directly on the rachis; several spikes may be clustered into a paniculate inflorescence
spikelet	basic unit of a grass flower, consisting of one to two glumes (bracts) at the base and one or more florets above
spp.	refers to multiple species of a single genus collectively
ssp.	subspecies; taxonomic rank below species
stamen	male, pollen-bearing organs of the flower
staminate	bearing stamens
sterile	lacking functional male and/or female flower parts; also used to describe lack of seed production
stolon	aboveground horizontal green stem that roots at the nodes
striate	marked with fine ± parallel lines
strict (contracted) panicle	panicle with branches that point upward instead of outward
subtend	lie underneath (e.g., "the lemma subtends the palea")
suffuse	gradually spread through or over
tawny	orange brown in color
terminal	borne at the end of a stem or branch, often contrasted with axillary
turgid	swollen
var.	variety; taxonomic rank below species and subspecies
vein	manifestation of the vascular tissue in a grass leaf or spikelet; may be impressed or raised (see also nerve)
vestigial	remnant of larger structure
winged	having one or more lateral parts, appendages, or projections

Parts of the Grass

Stems, Leaves, and Sheaths

The grass stem (culm) is jointed, comprising solid nodes and (usually) hollow internodes. Stems are generally round, but they can be flattened, as in *Panicum rigidulum* and *Poa compressa*. Grass leaves are differentiated into a blade and a sheath. The sheath is the lower portion of the leaf that surrounds the stem and is usually open (edges overlapping) in grasses; however, in some, such as *Bromus* and *Glyceria*, it is closed (edges united into a tube). The collar is where the blade meets the sheath, and it is marked by the ligule, found at the inside juncture of sheath and blade. The ligule is usually papery, it can also be reduced to a ring of hairs, and it is absent in some species. The collar may also have a pair of ear-like projections called auricles.

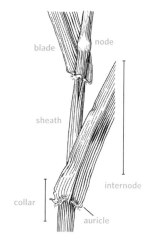

Cutaway of typical grass stem

Sheaths are typically categorized as open or closed. Open sheaths have overlapping edges for most of their length; the very bottom of the sheath may be united (as in *Dactylis glomerata*). In closed sheaths, the edges are united for more than one-half the length, forming a tube around the stem.

open sheath   closed sheath

The Grass Flower

The grass flower is called a floret and comprises a lemma (tougher outer bract) and a palea (delicate inner bract) that enclose the developing flower (stamens and pistil) and, eventually, the seed (caryopsis). The lemma is the more useful bract for keying, although the palea can be distinctive (i.e., in *Bromus* the margins are sometimes ciliate). Sometimes the palea is absent, as in some *Agrostis* species. The base of the lemma is called the callus. The callus ends in a sharp point and may be smooth, hairy (*Calamagrostis*) or bearded (*Muhlenbergia, Agrostis*).

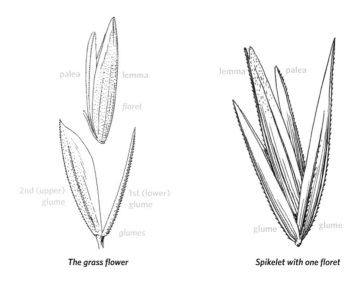

The grass flower

Spikelet with one floret

The floret(s) is subtended by two paired empty bracts called glumes. The first, or lower, glume is lower on the pedicel than the second, or upper, glume. The glumes can be longer than the floret (*Danthonia*), shorter (*Bromus, Festuca*), or even absent (*Leersia*). They can also be either nearly the same size or unequal, although the lower glume is usually smaller. Occasionally, the first glume is absent or extremely minute, as in some species of *Digitaria* and *Paspalum*. Sometimes there are sterile florets present with the fertile ones. Sterile florets are typically narrower (less plump) or generally smaller in size than fertile florets.

The glumes and the floret (lemma and palea) make up the spikelet. There can be one floret per spikelet or many florets per spikelet.

Spikelets with two to many florets

Disarticulation

When grasses mature, the inflorescence breaks apart (shatters) to disperse the seeds. If the florets fall without the accompanying glumes, the grass is said to disarticulate above the glumes. In this scenario, the glumes remain on the plant. If the florets and glumes fall as a single unit, the grass disarticulates below the glumes. Disarticulation is an important characteristic to consider when keying some grasses. Caution is required: in mature grasses, disarticulation of individual florets may make counting the number of florets per spikelet problematic. You should examine

Disarticulation above the glumes

Disarticulation below the glumes

more than one spikelet to confirm the identification. For grasses, you will only need to determine if a spikelet has one, two, or more than two florets.

To determine how the grass disarticulates, select a mature specimen and tug on a floret. If the floret is easily removed from the glumes, disarticulation is above the glumes. If tugging does not easily free the floret or results in the floret(s) and glumes coming off as a unit, disarticulation is below the glumes.

This drawing shows a spikelet with three florets artificially elongated to show the rachilla (the axis to which the florets are attached). When the floret disarticulates, the rachilla may stay attached to the floret below. In this situation, the rachilla is prolonged behind the palea. In spikelets with only one floret, a vestigial rachilla may be present (as in *Calamagrostis*).

Exploded spikelet showing rachilla

Roots and Rhizomes (Perennial versus Annual)

Grass keys often use belowground structures to differentiate species. Grasses that are perennial have tough, fibrous, deep roots, rhizomes, or stolons that permit the grass to survive year after year. Annual grasses

fibrous root system (annual)

rhizomatous (perennial)

typically have shallow, fibrous root systems that maintain the grass through the growing season but do not persist. The easiest way to tell whether a grass is perennial or annual is to pull it out of the ground, but only do this if there are several specimens and you do not suspect that the plant has special status (rare, threatened or endangered). If the grass comes out readily, it is an annual. If the grass is more stubborn, it is a perennial. Of course, the presence of rhizomes or stolons will also tell you that it is a perennial. Another nondestructive method of determining whether the grass is perennial or annual is to examine the stems (shoots). In annual plants, all of the stems produce flowers (referred to as fertile stems or shoots). In perennial plants, there will be non-flower producing (sterile) stems/shoots among the fertile stems.

Illustrated Characteristics of Grass Parts

Leaf and Sheath

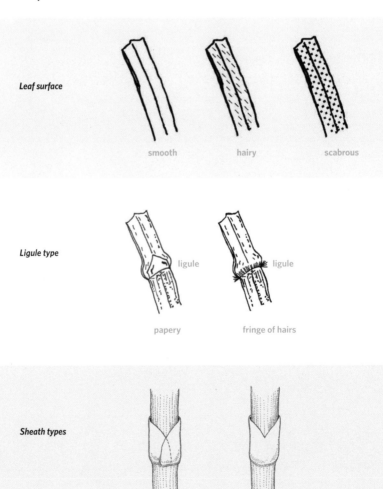

Leaf surface

smooth   hairy   scabrous

Ligule type

ligule   ligule

papery   fringe of hairs

Sheath types

open   closed

Inflorescence Types

Spike: unbranched inflorescence where the sessile spikelets sit directly on the rachis

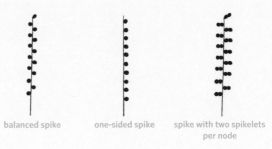

balanced spike

one-sided spike

spike with two spikelets per node

Raceme: elongate, unbranched inflorescence with pedicellate spikelets

raceme

raceme with spikelets on one side of the rachis

Panicle: elongate, branched inflorescence with pedicellate spikelets (main panicle branches are divided into smaller branchlets)

open panicle

lobe

strict (contracted) panicle

dense spikelike panicle

Digitate cluster: several branches arising from a single point (or approximate single point) like fingers on a hand

digitate cluster

approximate digitate cluster

Features of the Florets/Lemmas

Texture

hard

soft

Presence of awns

awned

awnless

Apex

forked (bifid)

blunt

pointed

Veins

conspicuous

obscure

Surface Features

Surface features

smooth

hairy all over

callus hairs

Surface features continued

bearded callus

web

scabrous

(rough to the touch due to short hairs or epidermis)

With sterile or rudimentary lemmas

fertile floret

sterile lemmas

rudimentary lemma

With sterile bristles

sterile bristle

Awn Types

Presence of awns

Awn: hairlike projection from the lemma or glumes that is actually an extension of a vein

Size

Number

Shape

Attachment location

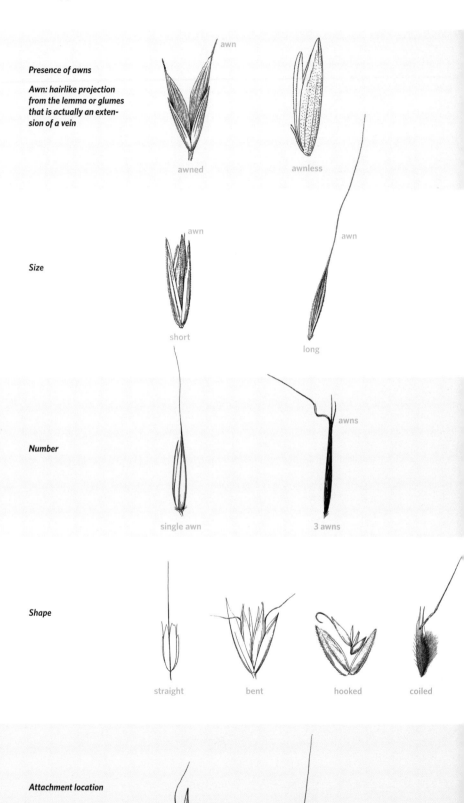

awn

awned

awnless

awn

awn

short

long

single awn

awns

3 awns

straight

bent

hooked

coiled

back of lemma

top of lemma

Some Unusual Grasses

The Rame

In a rame, the spikelets are paired at each node. The pair comprises a sessile, bisexual spikelet (usually awned) and a pedicellate spikelet that is (1) bisexual but reduced in size; (2) staminate; (3) sterile; or (4) reduced to just the pedicel. The rame is referred to as a triad when the pedicel supporting the spikelet above remains attached to the rame below. Most grasses with a rame-type arrangement are large (1–3 m tall).

Tip: Think hard glumes, soft lemmas.

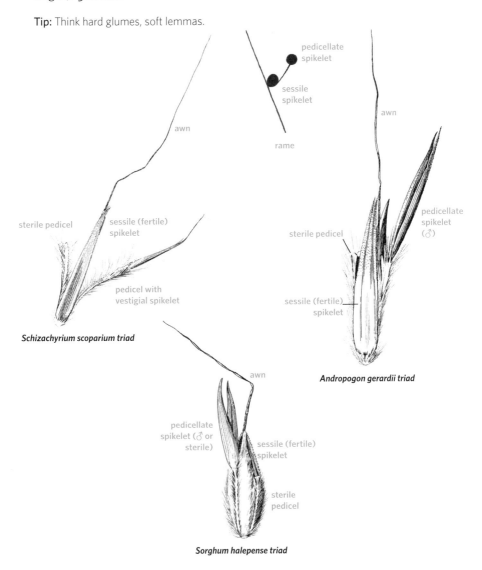

Schizachyrium scoparium triad

Andropogon gerardii triad

Sorghum halepense triad

Within each spikelet there are two lemmas. The lemmas are delicate and completely concealed by the hard, fused glumes; therefore, all you see are the glumes. The upper lemma is fertile and awned (the awn extends through a pore in the top of the glumes and is visible). The lower lemma is either sterile or empty.

Phalaridae Tribe

Anthoxanthum and *Phalaris* are members of the Phalaridae tribe characterized by a unique spikelet structure. In these grasses, the glumes completely enclose the single fertile floret, which itself is subtended by a pair of staminate or sterile lemmas (when the palea is not present). In *Anthoxanthum*, the sterile lemmas are longer than the fertile floret. In *Phalaris*, the sterile lemmas are smaller than the fertile floret.

Tip: To examine the florets, you need to tease them out of the glumes.

sterile lemmas

spikelet (side view) fertile floret

Anthoxanthum odoratum

fertile floret fertile floret

staminate lemmas spikelet

Anthoxanthum nitens

fertile lemma

sterile lemma

glumes

Phalaris arundinacea

fertile floret

sterile lemma

spikelet

Phalaris canariensis

Paniceae Tribe

Grasses in the Paniceae tribe have a specialized flower structure. The spikelet is comprised of two glumes, a sterile lemma, and a fertile lemma. The first glume is short (or absent); the second glume is as long as the entire floret; the sterile lemma is equal to the second glume in appearance, texture, and size. (Hence the flower will appear to have three glumes!) The fertile lemma is hard and shiny (*Panicum, Echinochloa, Paspalum, Eriochloa villosa*) or leathery in texture (*Digitaria*). In some cases (*Digitaria, Eriochloa villosa, Paspalum,* and some species of *Panicum*), the first glume is lacking, or minute, and the second glume and sterile lemma appear as two glumes.

Tip: Think hard lemmas, soft glumes.

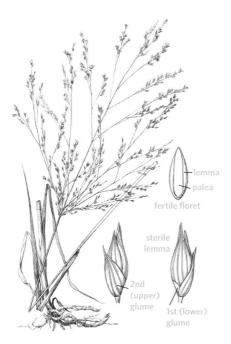

lemma
palea
fertile floret

sterile lemma

2nd (upper) glume

1st (lower) glume

Panicum virgatum

sterile bristles

sterile lemma
1st (lower) glume

2nd (upper) glume

lemma palea

fertile floret

Setaria magna

Echinochloa crus-galli

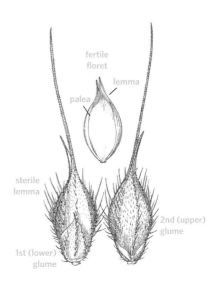

fertile floret

lemma

palea

sterile lemma

2nd (upper) glume

1st (lower) glume

General Key

To use this dichotomous key,

(1) read the choices;

(2) select the phrase that best describes the
grass specimen in question;

(3) follow that branch in the key. Repeat these
steps until the grass has been identified.

If the grass stems are woody or woodylike and the grass is large (typically over 3 m in height), go to

below

If the grass is herbaceous (green, non-woody) and smaller in stature, go to

below

If the stems are woody and the leaves are arranged in fan-shaped clusters at the tips of new stems (topknots), it is *Arundinaria gigantea* (river cane, giant cane). Damp woods, wet ground, swamps; inland.

If the stems are woodylike and the leaves arise singly from the stem, go to

page 19

Arundinaria gigantea

Arundinaria tecta

Note: Some treatments recognize a second species of *Arundinaria*, which is *A. tecta* (switch cane). Damp woods, wet ground; coastal. It is distinguished from *A. gigantea* by the presence of leaves along the stem. *A. gigantea* has deciduous stem leaves; *A. tecta* has stem leaves that are persistent to tardily deciduous.

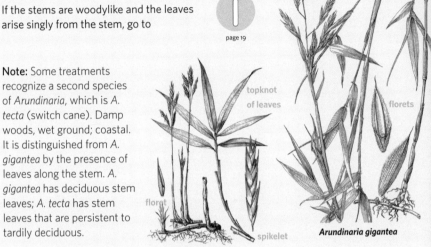

persistent sheath

topknot of leaves

florets

floret

spikelet

Arundinaria tecta

Arundinaria gigantea

If the flowers are enclosed in sharp, spiny burs and . . .

the burs are 3–4 mm long, including spines, it is *Tragus racemosus*† (stalked burgrass). Roadsides, disturbed areas, ballast.

the burs are 8–15 mm long, including spines, it is *Cenchrus* (sandbur). See page 98.

Tragus racemosus

If the flowers are not enclosed in spiny burs, go to

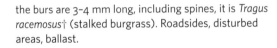

page 19

bur

Tragus racemosus

bur

Cenchrus tribuloides

bur

spikelet

Cenchrus spinifex

If the plants are tall (3–10 m) and the inflorescence is whitish when mature, it is *Arundo donax*† (giant cane). Disturbed areas.

Arundo donax

If the plants are smaller in height (2–4 m) and the inflorescence is tawny when mature, it is *Phragmites* (common reed).

Phragmites australis ssp. *americanus*

Phragmites australis ssp. *americanus*: the stems are smooth, shiny, and red to dark brown to green with frequent dark fungal spots; ligules 0.4–0.9 mm long. Freshwater marshes; FACW.

Phragmites australis ssp. *australis*

Phragmites australis ssp. *australis*†: the stems are rough and dull tan to green without frequent dark fungal spots; ligules 1–1.7 mm long. Marshes; FACW.

Tip: How to distinguish native giant cane / switchcane from ornamental bamboos: bamboos have one branch per node (*Pseudosasa japonica*) or consistently two branches per node; they rarely have a smaller central third branch (*Phyllostachys* spp.). Native canes typically have two to seven branches per node.

floret

spikelet

Arundo donax

floret

spikelet

Phragmites australis

Poa bulbosa

If some or all of the flowers are modified into purplish bulblets with long pointed tips, it is *Poa bulbosa*† (bulbous bluegrass). Waste ground; FACU.

If the flowers are not modified into bulblets, go to

page 20

bulblet

Poa bulbosa

If the rachis is evidently thickened, with spikelets sunken into the hollows along its length (in *Tripsacum*, only the ♀ spikelets are sunken), go to

below

If the rachis is thin and the spikelets are not sunken, go to

page 21

Grass inflorescence with thin rachis, spikelets not sunken

 If the plant is small (3–7 dm tall) and the glumes are awned, it is the weed *Aegilops cylindrica*† (jointed goatgrass). Disturbed habitats.

Aegilops cylindrica

If the plant is large (1–3 m tall) and the glumes are awnless, it is *Tripsacum dactyloides* (Eastern gamagrass). Roadsides, moist areas, disturbed areas; FAC/FACW.

Tripsacum dactyloides

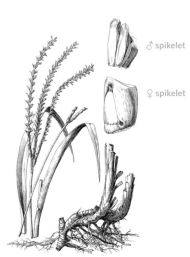

♂ spikelet

♀ spikelet

Tripsacum dactyloides

thickened rachis

Aegilops cylindrica

If the grass is typically a straggling annual with leaves having shiny, silvery, and slightly off-center midveins, it is *Microstegium vimineum*† (Nepalese browntop, Japanese stiltgrass). Disturbed areas; FAC.

Note: *Microstegium* may reach heights of > 2 m when it climbs up other vegetation.

icrostegium vimineum

If the grass is a low-growing and straggling perennial with leaf blades that are horizontally rippled or undulating, flowering late summer into fall, it is *Oplismenus hirtellus*† [*O. undulatifolius*] (bristle basketgrass). Forests and shell middens in the coastal plain; FAC/FACU.

Oplismenus hirtellus

If the leaves are not as above, and the plant is an annual or perennial, go to

below

Note: *Microstegium* is a very aggressive weed, often growing in dense patches along shady paths and in disturbed areas; the flowers appear late in the season (September to early November), so the leaves are often all you see.

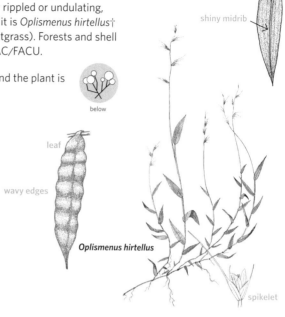

inflorescence

Microstegium vimineum

leaf

shiny midrib

leaf

wavy edges

Oplismenus hirtellus

spikelet

If the inflorescence is a panicle that is dense and spikelike, go to

page 65

Tip: Dense, spikelike panicles have branches, but they are so compact that it is hard to see them. If you can easily see branching, it is not a dense, spikelike panicle.

If the inflorescence is a spike, raceme, strict (contacted) to open panicle, or digitate cluster (see below), go to

page 22

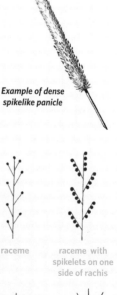

Example of dense spikelike panicle

Tip: If the spikelets are sessile—that is, attached directly to the rachis—it is a spike, not a spikelike panicle. To tell if the spikelets are sessile, it is usually easiest to look at the lowermost ones. Also, a "strict" panicle may appear spikelike, but strict panicles will have lobes.

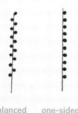

balanced spike

one-sided spike

spike with two spikelets per node

raceme

raceme with spikelets on one side of rachis

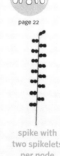

open panicle

strict (contracted) panicle

digitate cluster

approximate digitate cluster

If the grass is > 2 m tall, go to

below

If the grass is < 2 m tall, go to

page 27

 If the inflorescence is a digitate cluster, go to

below

If the inflorescence is a dense, strict (contracted) or open panicle or raceme (single or paired), go to

page 23

 If the inflorescence is terminal and solitary on each stem and the spikelets are somewhat concealed by long silky hairs (either silvery to grayish or tawny to purplish), it is *Miscanthus sinensis*† (eulalia). Cultivated and escaped to roadsides; upland (UPL)/FACU.

Miscanthus sinensis

If the inflorescence consists of usually more than one digitate cluster per stem and the rachis and pedicels are usually hairy (but the hairs are not concealing the spikelets), it is *Andropogon* (bluestem). See page 84.

spikelet

Miscanthus sinensis

spikelet pair

Andropogon gerardii

If the ligule is split like this, it is *Sorghastrum nutans* (Indian grass). Moist or dry woodlands and forests, roadsides; FACU.

Sorghastrum nutans

If the ligule is membranous (may or may not have a fringe of hairs) or reduced to a ring of hairs, go to

below

split ligule

awn

spikelet

Sorghastrum nutans

If the inflorescence comprises several paired racemes, it is *Andropogon* (bluestem). See page 84.

If the inflorescence comprises a dense, strict (contracted) or open panicle or raceme, go to

page 24

Paired racemes of Andropogon

If the spikelets are arranged on two sides of a triangular rachis, and this is a plant of brackish and freshwater marshes, it is *Spartina* (cordgrass). See page 153.

If the rachis is not triangular (plants of various habitats), go to

below

Spartina cynosuroides

floret spi

If the inflorescence is a dense, compact panicle, go to

below

If the inflorescence is a strict (contracted) to open panicle, go to

page 25

If the upper leaves are spathelike, enclosing the peduncle and the base of the racemes, it is *Andropogon* (bluestem). See page 84.

If the upper leaves are not spathelike and do not enclose the peduncle and the base of the racemes, go to

page 25

spikelet

Andropogon glomeratus

spathe

inflorescence

If the spikelets are paired at each node, with one sessile and one pedicellate spikelet (rame) that are both fertile and alike in size, it is *Saccharum* [*Erianthus*] (plumegrass). Some species also have a ring of hairs at each node of the stem. See page 148.

If the spikelets are paired at each node, with one sessile and one pedicellate spikelet (rame), and the pedicellate spikelet is staminate or sterile and smaller than the sessile spikelet, it is *Sorghum*† (sorghum). See page 152.

Note: See page 13 for more information on rames.

Tip: *Sorghum* leaves have a distinctive white, tan, or brown midrib.

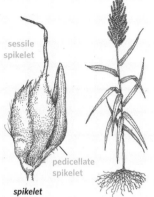

sessile spikelet

pedicellate spikelet

spikelet

Sorghum bicolor

spikelet

Saccharum giganteum

If the spikelets are paired at each node, with one sessile and one pedicellate spikelet, and the pedicellate spikelet is staminate or sterile and smaller than the sessile spikelet, it is *Sorghum*† (Johnsongrass). See page 152.

If the spikelets are single at each node, go to

below

spikelet

Sorghum halepense

If the ♂ and ♀ spikelets are separate, but on the same inflorescence (♂ and ♀ spikelets will look different); large aquatic grasses, go to

page 26

If the spikelets are perfect (♂ and ♀ parts are not on separate spikelets on the same plant, and all the spikelets look alike), plants of various habitats, go to

page 26

If the ♀ spikelets are in a large spray at the top of the inflorescence and the ♂ spikelets are drooping below, it is *Zizania* (wildrice). See page 159.

Zizaniopsis miliacea

If the ♀ and ♂ spikelets are intermixed within the inflorescence, it is *Zizaniopsis miliacea* (giant cutgrass). Brackish and freshwater marshes; OBL.

♀

♂

inflorescence

Zizania

♂

♀

spikelets

♀ spikelet (2 views)   ♂ spikelet

Zizaniopsis miliacea

If there is a single hard fertile floret per spikelet, go to

page 27

Uniola paniculata

If there are ten or more fertile florets per spikelet, it is *Uniola paniculata* (sea oats). Beach sands, dunes; FACW.

floret

Uniola paniculata

If the surface of the hard fertile floret is hairy and there are two tufts of hairs at the base (sterile lemmas, so use a hand lens to see), it is *Phalaris* (canarygrass). See page 142.

If the surface of the hard fertile floret is smooth, it is *Panicum* (panicgrass). See page 135.

fertile floret

sterile lemma

glumes

Phalaris arundinacea

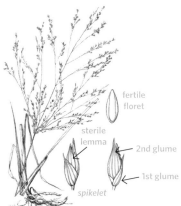

fertile floret

sterile lemma

2nd glume

1st glume

spikelet

Panicum virgatum

If the inflorescence is a spike, like one of these, go to

page 60

two-sided spike with one spikelet per node

one-sided spike

two-sided spike with two spikelets per node

Spikes

If the inflorescence is a digitate cluster (or more or less digitate in appearance), with three or more branches arising from a common point, like fingers on a hand, go to

page 62

digitate cluster

approximate digitate cluster

Digitate clusters

If the inflorescence is an open to strict (contracted) raceme or panicle or paired racemes, go to

page 28

Tip: To tell if the spikelets are sessile, it is usually easiest to look at the lowermost ones.

Tip: Do I have a panicle or a spike? A panicle is a branched inflorescence with spikelets on pedicels. A spike is an inflorescence with sessile spikelets along an elongate axis.

raceme

raceme (spikelets on one side of rachis)

Racemes

open panicle

strict (contracted) panicle

Panicles

If the inflorescence is spikelike with many (twenty-five to forty) dangling smaller spikes that are widely spaced on ± one side of the rachis (note short curved pedicels), it is *Bouteloua curtipendula* (sideoats grama). Serpentine barrens, dry calcareous clearings, and other dry, rocky, sandy sites.

Bouteloua curtipendula

If the inflorescence is not as above, go to

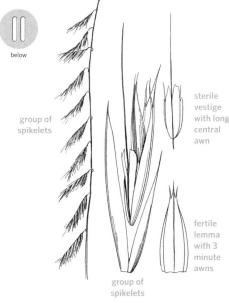

below

sterile vestige with long central awn

group of spikelets

fertile lemma with 3 minute awns

group of spikelets

Bouteloua curtipendula

If the panicle branches are few and widely spaced, with the lowest branch pointing stiffly upward (or sometimes at a right angle to the stem), the spikelets are in one-sided clusters (glomerules) at the tips of the panicle branches, the stem is flattened at the base, and the sheath is partially closed, it is *Dactylis glomerata†* (orchard grass). Fields, pastures, meadows, roadsides; common; FACU.

Dactylis glomerata

If the plant is not as above, go to

page 29

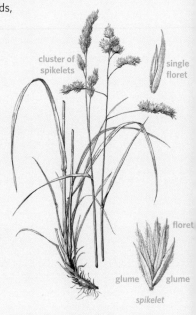

cluster of spikelets

single floret

floret

glume   glume

spikelet

Dactylis glomerata

If there is a pair of spikelets (one sessile and one pedicellate) at each node of the inflorescence branches (rame; see below and on page 13), go to

page 32

Note: Examples of rames shown here.

If there is only one spikelet per node (in other words, not a rame), go to

below

Tip: Most grasses with a rame-type inflorescence are large grasses > 1 m tall.

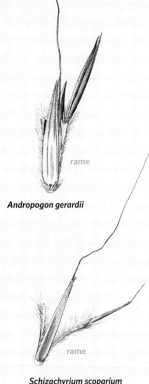

rame

Andropogon gerardii

rame

Schizachyrium scoparium

If the single awnless fertile floret is underlain by two hairy awned or awnless sterile/staminate lemmas (in *Phalaris*, these resemble tufts of hair), go to

page 30

If there are no paired sterile or staminate lemmas beneath the single awned or awnless fertile floret (and the floret is hard, leathery, or papery), or there are two to many florets, go to

page 31

If the sterile lemmas are longer than and enclose the fertile floret, it is *Anthoxanthum* (vernalgrass). See page 85.

If the sterile lemmas are shorter than the fertile floret, it is *Phalaris* (canarygrass). See page 142.

Note: See page 14 for more information on these grasses.

Anthoxanthum nitens

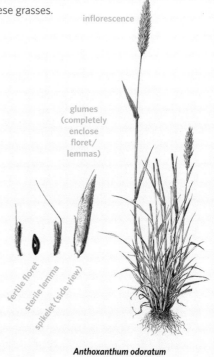

inflorescence

glumes (completely enclose floret/ lemmas)

fertile floret

sterile lemma

spikelet (side view)

Anthoxanthum odoratum

fertile floret

sterile lemmas

glumes

Phalaris arundinacea

fertile floret

sterile lemmas

glumes

Phalaris canariensis

If the spikelet comprises a first glume, a second glume, a glumelike sterile lemma, and a hard fertile floret (examine with a hand lens), it is one of these grasses: *Dichanthelium*, *Digitaria cognata* (first glume very short or lacking), *Echinochloa*, *Eriochloa villosa*† (first glume obsolete), *Panicum*, *Paspalum* (first glume very short or lacking), *Pennisetum alopecuroides*†, *Sacciolepis striata*, *Setaria*, or *Urochloa*. Go to

page 72

If the spikelet is not arranged in this fashion, go to

page 32

Tip: Think hard lemmas, soft glumes.

Note: See page 15 for more information on these grasses.

Echinochloa crus-galli

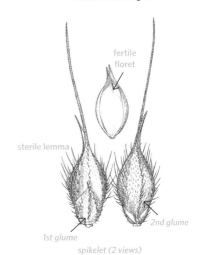

fertile floret

sterile lemma

1st glume

2nd glume

spikelet (2 views)

Echinochloa crus-galli

Eriochloa villosa

cuplike structure

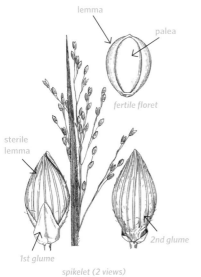

lemma

palea

fertile floret

sterile lemma

1st glume

2nd glume

spikelet (2 views)

Panicum

spikelet

Paspalum

sterile bristle

spikelet

fertile floret

Setaria

If the inflorescence is an open panicle and the ♂ and ♀ spikelets are separate, but on the same inflorescence (♂ and ♀ spikelets will look different); large, aquatic grasses, and . . .

> the ♀ flowers are in a large spray at the top and the ♂ flowers dangle from the lower branches, it is *Zizania* (wildrice). See page 159.

> the ♀ and ♂ spikelets are intermixed within the inflorescence, it is *Zizaniopsis miliacea* (giant cutgrass). See page 26.

If the inflorescence is a dense, strict (contracted) or open panicle or raceme and the fertile spikelets are perfect (i.e., each spikelet has both ♂ and ♀ parts, and all the spikelets look alike), go to

page 34

If the ligule is split, it is *Sorghastrum nutans* (Indian grass). See page 23.

If the ligule is membranous or hairy (not split), go to

page 33

If the inflorescence comprises several solitary racemes, it is *Schizachyrium scoparium* (little bluestem). Dry soils, old fields, prairies, open woods, coastal sands; FACU.

Schizachyrium scoparium

If the inflorescence comprises several paired racemes, it is *Andropogon* (bluestem). Go to page 84.

If the inflorescence is a dense, strict (contracted) or open panicle or paired racemes, go to

page 24

solitary raceme

spikelet

Schizachyrium scoparium

paired racemes

dense panicle

open panicle

If there is one floret per pair of glumes, go to

below

If there is more than one floret per pair of glumes, go to

page 43

If there are no glumes present, it is *Leersia* (cutgrass); note that there are rough leaves on some species. See page 127.

Note: Grasses with one floret per pair of glumes often have sterile lemma(s) associated with them. The sterile lemma(s) can be above the fertile floret, as in *Melica*, or below, as in *Anthoxanthum* and *Panicum*.

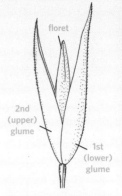

floret

2nd (upper) glume

1st (lower) glume

One floret per pair of glumes

floret

overlapping florets

Leersia oryzoides. In this genus, the floret sits in a tiny cup at the top of the pedicel. The glumes are absent.

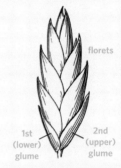

florets

1st (lower) glume

2nd (upper) glume

2 or more florets per pair of glumes

If the lemma has at least one awn or is awn-tipped, go to

page 35

If the lemma is awnless, go to

page 41

awn

lemma

palea

glumes

Cinna spikelet

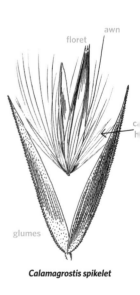

awn

floret

glumes

Calamagrostis spikelet

If the lemma has only one awn, go to

below

If the lemma has three awns, it is *Aristida* (threeawn).
See page 87.

Tip: Be careful. Sometimes
the awns can be minute, as
in *Cinna*, or hidden by hairs,
as in *Calamagrostis*.

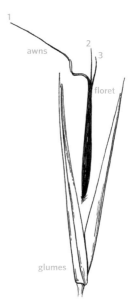

Aristida dichotoma spikelet

If the awn is elongated (> 5 mm long), go to

page 36

If the awn is short (< 5 mm long), go to

page 37

If the awn is coiled or twisted at the base, go to

below

If the awn is not coiled (may be wavy or bent), go to

page 39

Examples of long awns

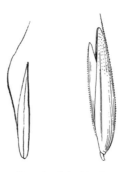

Examples of short awns

If the awn is readily detached, it is *Piptatherum* (piptatherum, ricegrass). See page 142.

If the awn is firmly attached, go to

page 37

floret

glumes

Piptatherum canadense

If the edges of the dark brown lemma curl over the margins of the palea, leaving it exposed, it is *Piptochaetium avenaceum* (blackseed speargrass). Upland woodlands, forests.

If the edges of the brown lemma overlap, concealing most of the palea, it is *Hesperostipa spartea* (porcupine grass). Roadsides.

Hesperostipa spartea

coiled
awn

callus
hairs

floret

Piptochaetium avenaceum

coiled
awn

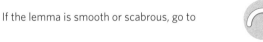

floret

glumes

Hesperostipa spartea [Stipa spartea]

If any part of the lemma is hairy, go to

page 38

If the lemma is smooth or scabrous, go to

page 38

If the lemma has a tuft of straight, stiff, white hairs arising from the base (callus hairs) and the hairs are . . .

one-half the length to > the length of the lemma, it is *Calamagrostis* (reedgrass). See page 96.

< one-half the length of the lemma (*Agrostis* or *Muhlenbergia*), go to

page 43

If the entire lemma is covered with short, appressed hairs, it is *Piptatherum* (piptatherum, ricegrass). See page 142.

callus hairs

floret

awn

spikelet

Calamagrostis canadensis

awn

Piptatherum pungens

floret

If the floret disarticulates below the glumes, it is *Cinna* (woodreed). See page 99.

If the floret disarticulates above the glumes, it is *Muhlenbergia* (muhly). See page 130.

Tip: Many *Muhlenbergia* have scaly rhizomes.

glumes

floret

minute awn

floret

glumes

floret

floret

glumes

Cinna arundinacea

Muhlenbergia capillaris   **Cinna latifolia**

If the floret is > the glumes in length, go to

below

If the floret ≤ the glumes in length, go to

page 40

If the entire lemma is hairy, it is *Brachyelytrum* (shorthusk). See page 89.

If the lemma is smooth, rough to the touch, or sparsely hairy only at the base (bearded callus), go to

page 40

Tip: *Brachyelytrum*s are forest grasses.

hairy on veins

floret

glumes

Brachyelytrum erectum

If the entire lemma is hairy, go to

page 41

If the lemma is smooth or hairy only at the base (bearded callus) and . . .

the lemma is conspicuously three-veined, it is *Muhlenbergia* (muhly). See page 130.

the lemma is five-veined (veins faint to sharp) or obscurely veined, it is *Agrostis* (bentgrass). See page 78.

floret

spikelet
(2 views)

Muhlenbergia sylvatica

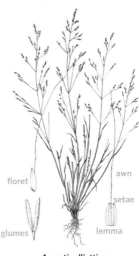

floret

awn

setae

glumes

lemma

Agrostis elliottiana

If the rachilla is prolonged behind the palea, it is *Brachyelytrum* (shorthusk). See page 89.

If the rachilla is not prolonged behind the palea, it is *Muhlenbergia* (muhly). See page 130.

Brachyelytrum aristosum

awn

rachilla

floret

floret

spikelet

Muhlenbergia tenuiflora

If the lemma wraps around and completely conceals the palea, and the upper stem leaves are reduced or bladeless, it is *Oryzopsis asperifolia* (roughleaf ricegrass). High elevation pine–oak / heath barrens and woodlands.

Oryzopsis asperifolia

If the palea is exposed and the upper stem leaves are prominent, it is *Piptatherum* (piptatherum, ricegrass). See page 142.

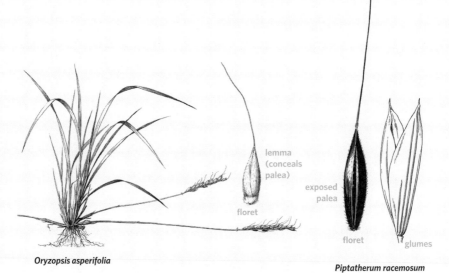

lemma
(conceals
palea)

floret

exposed
palea

floret

glumes

Oryzopsis asperifolia

Piptatherum racemosum

If the inflorescence is one-sided, and this is a plant of fresh and salt marshes, it is *Spartina* (cordgrass). See page 153.

If the inflorescence is balanced (on both sides of the rachis), go to

page 42

one-sided

Spartina patens

If the lemma has a tuft of straight, stiff, white hairs arising from the base (callus hairs) that are one-half the length of the lemma to > its length, ± concealing the lemma, it is *Calamovilfa* (sandreed). See page 98.

Note: *Calamagrostis* will key here if you miss the awn. See page 96.

If the lemma is smooth or variously hairy, but not as above, go to

below

callus hairs

floret

spikelet

Calamovilfa longifolia

If the lemma is firm, smooth, white, and shiny at maturity, it is *Milium effusum* (wood millet). Rare in forests at high to moderate elevations; FACU.

Milium effusum

If the lemma is leathery and the inflorescence is a large, diffuse panicle, often one-third to one-half the height of the plant, it is *Digitaria cognata* [*Leptoloma cognatum*] (fall witchgrass). Sandy fields and roadsides.

Digitaria cognata

If the lemma is delicate, soft, and papery, go to

page 43

Tip: Three other grasses may key here if you miss certain features: (1) *Eriochloa villosa* (page 31) if you miss the cuplike structure at the base of the floret; (2) *Phalaris arundinacea* (page 142) if you miss the sterile lemmas at the base of the floret; and (3) *Cinna* (page 99) if you miss the minute awn.

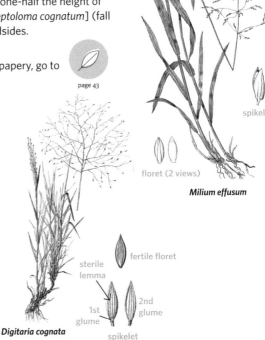

spikelet

floret (2 views)

Milium effusum

sterile lemma

fertile floret

1st glume

2nd glume

spikelet

Digitaria cognata

If both glumes are shorter than the floret, or one glume is shorter and one is as long or longer than the floret, and . . .

    the lemma is one-veined (and the seeds usually gelatinize when wet), it is *Sporobolus* (dropseed). See page 155.

    the lemma is conspicuously three-veined, it is *Muhlenbergia* (muhly). See page 130.

If both glumes are equal to or longer than the floret and . . .

    the lemma is five-veined (veins faint to sharp) or obscurely veined, it is *Agrostis* (bentgrass). See page 78.

    the lemma is conspicuously three-veined, it is *Muhlenbergia* (muhly). See page 130.

Tip: The seeds of most species of *Sporobolus* gelatinize when wet.

floret
glumes
spikelet
tuft of white hairs

Sporobolus cryptandrus

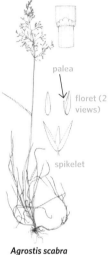

palea
floret (2 views)
spikelet

Agrostis scabra

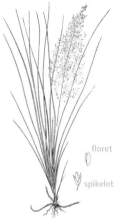

floret
spikelet

Muhlenbergia torreyana

If the lemmas have cobwebby hairs at the base, it is *Poa* (bluegrass). See page 143.

If there are no cobwebby hairs at the base of the lemma, go to

page 44

Tip: Only two *Poas* (*P. annua* and *P. autumnalis*) do not have cobwebby hairs at the base of the lemma, so this is a pretty good way to tell if you have a *Poa*. Also, in *Poas*, the tips of the leaves come together like the prow of a canoe. This is a good way to identify a *Poa* vegetatively.

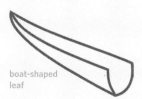

boat-shaped leaf

floret
cobwebby hairs

Poa

43

If the glumes are collectively shorter than the lemmas, go to

below

If at least one glume is about as long as the spikelet, or longer (not including the awns), go to

page 53

If the veins of the lemma are evident to prominent (use a hand lens), go to

below

If the veins are obscure, go to

page 52

Tip: How to count veins: first, count the number of veins on the side facing you. Then double the number (for those on the other side you can't see) and add one (for the central vein on the keel).

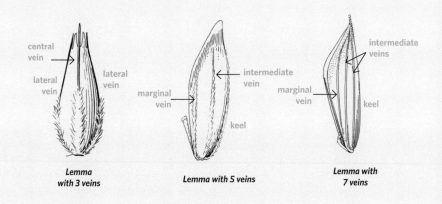

Lemma with 3 veins

central vein

lateral vein

lateral vein

Lemma with 5 veins

marginal vein

intermediate vein

keel

Lemma with 7 veins

intermediate veins

marginal vein

keel

If the lemma has three prominent veins (in *Eragrostis*, sometimes the lateral ones may be obscure), go to

page 45

If the lemma has five or more usually conspicuous veins, go to

page 47

If the mature spikelets have stiff, large, protruding, bottle-shaped seeds and the inflorescence has appressed branches, it is *Diarrhena* (beakgrain). See page 102.

If there are no protruding, bottle-shaped seeds, the seeds are small and inconspicuous, and the inflorescence is an open panicle, go to

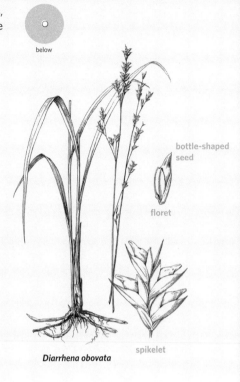

below

bottle-shaped seed

floret

spikelet

Diarrhena obovata

If the spikelets are on one side of the rachis, it is *Leptochloa* (sprangletop). See page 128.

If the spikelets are on both sides of the rachis, go to

page 46

Leptochloa fusca
(spikelets all on one side)

If the plant is a low-growing, creeping annual, forming large mats on the soil surface, it is *Eragrostis* (lovegrass). See page 116.

If the plant is erect, not mat forming, and is an annual or a perennial, go to

below

If the lemmas are smooth, it is *Eragrostis* (lovegrass). See page 116.

If the lemmas are hairy, go to

below

Tip: *Eragrostis* species typically have many lemmas.

If the tip of the lemma has two rounded lobes with an awn between them, and the upper half of the palea is densely hairy (infloresences are mostly included in the upper sheaths), it is *Triplasis purpurea* (purple sandgrass). Dunes, maritime dry grasslands, open sandy areas; common.

Triplasis purpurea

If the tip of the lemma has two pointed teeth with a short awn between them, the palea is smooth to short-haired, the grasses are tall with a large exerted panicle, and the upper stem and panicle branches are greasy-sticky when mature, it is *Tridens flavus* (purpletop tridens, greasegrass). Roadsides, disturbed areas, glades; common; FACU.

Tridens flavus

floret

palea

lemma

spikelet

Triplasis purpurea

floret

palea

spikelet

Tridens flavus

If the edges of the leaf sheath are united (closed), (check more than one), go to

below

If the edges of the leaf sheath overlap for ± their entire length (open), (check more than one), go to

page 49

Tip: Sometimes a united sheath can split down the middle—but the edges still will not overlap.

Closed sheath

Open sheath

If lemmas are awned, go to

below

If lemmas are awnless, go to

page 48

If spikelets are three- to five-flowered, the glumes are purple at the base, and the panicle branches have few (one to three) spikelets each, it is *Schizachne purpurascens* (false melic). Rare in moist, rocky northern hardwood and spruce forests; FACU.

If the spikelets are several- to many-flowered, the glumes are green, yellow, or brown at the base, and the panicles have many spikelets, it is *Bromus* (brome). See page 90.

Schizachne purpurascens

Tip: *Schizachne* and *Danthonia* are similar in appearance, but in *Schizachne*, the glumes are < the florets in length; in *Danthonia*, the glumes are > the florets in length.

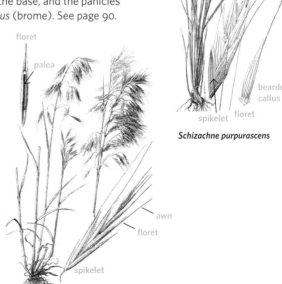

floret

palea

floret

bearded callus

spikelet   floret

Schizachne purpurascens

awn

floret

spikelet

Bromus tectorum

47

If the uppermost lemma(s) are smaller and sterile, it is *Melica* (melic). See page 129.

If all the lemmas are similar in size and fertile, go to

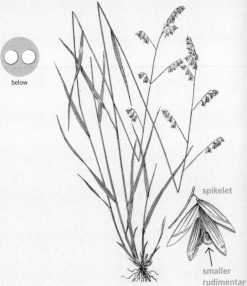

spikelet

smaller rudimentar floret

Melica mutica

If the second glume is one-veined, and this is a plant of wet habitats, it is *Glyceria* (mannagrass). See page 123.

If the second glume is three- to seven-veined, and this is a plant of drier habitats, it is *Bromus* (brome). See page 90.

Tip: All *Glyceria* species are wetland plants, and most have very distinct veins on the lemmas, so if you are in a wetland, think *Glyceria*.

Tip: To easily tell *Bromus* and *Festuca* apart, examine the sheath. *Bromus* has a closed sheath and *Festuca* an open sheath.

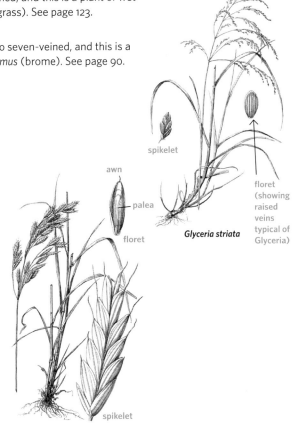

awn

palea

floret

spikelet

spikelet

floret (showing raised veins typical of Glyceria)

Glyceria striata

Bromus secalinus

If the spikelets are about as long as they are wide, it is *Briza* † (quakinggrass). See page 90.

If the spikelets are longer than they are wide, go to

below

spikelet

floret

Briza minor

If the leaf blades are strongly to ± curled under, and this is a plant of salt marshes, beaches, and dunes, go to

below

If the leaf blades are flat or curled under (plants of various habitats), go to

page 50

If the plant is low-growing (1.5–4 dm tall) and the leaf blades are strongly curled under, it is *Distichlis spicata* (salt-grass). Tidal brackish high marshes; OBL/FACW.

Distichlis spicata

If the plant is tall (1–2.5 m) and the leaf blades are ± curled under, it is *Uniola paniculata* (sea oats). Beach sands, dunes; FACW. See page 26.

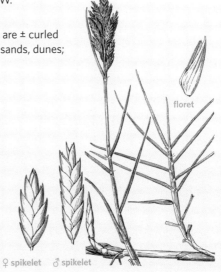

floret

♀ spikelet   ♂ spikelet

Distichlis spicata

If the lemmas are blunt at the tip, not awned and parallel veined, go to

below

If the lemmas are pointed (may have two teeth at the tip) or awned and the veins converge, go to

below

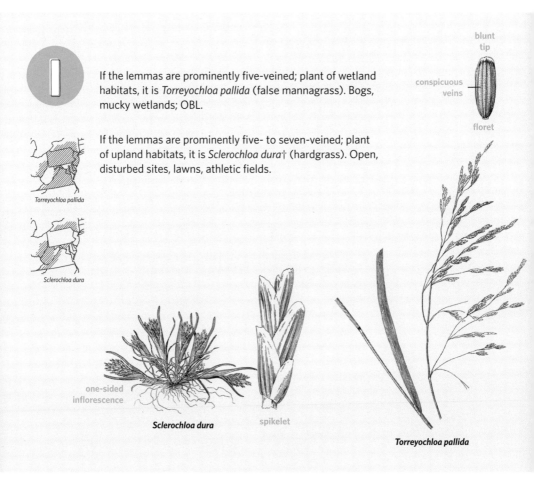

If the lemmas are prominently five-veined; plant of wetland habitats, it is *Torreyochloa pallida* (false mannagrass). Bogs, mucky wetlands; OBL.

If the lemmas are prominently five- to seven-veined; plant of upland habitats, it is *Sclerochloa dura†* (hardgrass). Open, disturbed sites, lawns, athletic fields.

blunt tip

conspicuous veins

floret

Torreyochloa pallida

Sclerochloa dura

one-sided inflorescence

Sclerochloa dura

spikelet

Torreyochloa pallida

If the lemmas are awned, go to

page 51

If the lemmas are not awned, go to

page 51

If the plant is an erect perennial, it is *Festuca/Schedonorus* (fescue). See page 120.

If the plant is a prostrate annual, it is *Vulpia* (fescue). See page 158.

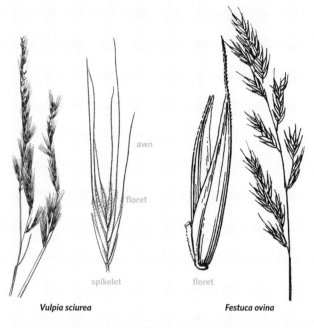

Vulpia sciurea

Festuca ovina

If the spikelets are flattened, it is *Chasmanthium* (river oats, chasmanthium). See page 99.

If the spikelets are not flattened, go to

page 52

Chasmanthium laxum

Chasmanthium latifolium

If the keel of the lemma is hairy, it is *Poa* (bluegrass; spp. with no web). See page 143.

If the keel of the lemma is not hairy, it is *Festuca/Schedonorus* (fescue). See page 120.

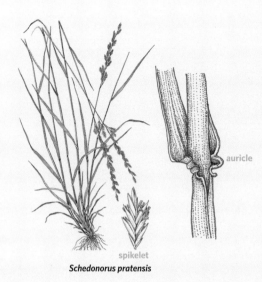

auricle

spikelet

Schedonorus pratensis

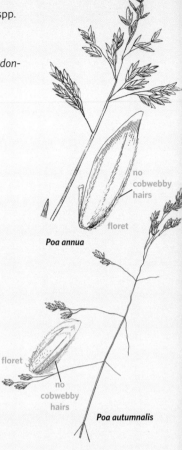

no cobwebby hairs

floret

Poa annua

floret

no cobwebby hairs

Poa autumnalis

If the lemmas are blunt at the tip, it is *Puccinellia* (alkali grass). See page 148.

If the lemmas are pointed or awned at the tip, go to

page 53

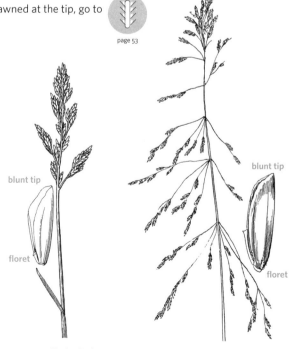

blunt tip

floret

Puccinellia fasciculata

blunt tip

floret

Puccinellia distans

If the spikelets disarticulate above the glumes, go to

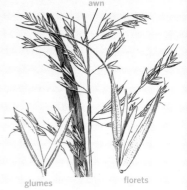

below

If the spikelets disarticulate below the glumes, it is *Sphenopholis* (wedgegrass). See page 154.

awn

glumes   florets

Sphenopholis pensylvanica

If the plant is an erect perennial, it is *Festuca/Schedonorus* (fescue). See page 120.

If the plant is a prostrate annual, it is *Vulpia* (fescue). See page 158.

awn

glumes   florets

Vulpia myuros

If the spikelets are big (2 cm long or greater), it is *Avena*† (oat). See page 89.

If the spikelets are smaller, go to

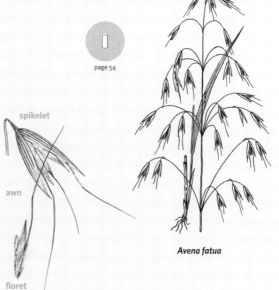

page 54

spikelet

awn

floret

Avena fatua

If there are two florets per pair of glumes, go to

below

If there are more than two florets per pair of glumes, go to

page 55

 If the lemmas are awnless, go to

below

If at least one lemma is awned, go to

page 55

 If the spikelets are on both sides of the rachis, go to

page 55

If the spikelets are on one side of an elongate rachis, it is *Leptochloa* (sprangletop). See page 128.

spikelets on one side of rachis

floret

spikelet

Leptochloa

If both lemmas are awned, go to

page 56

If only one lemma is awned, go to

page 58

If the florets disarticulate above the glumes, it is *Koeleria macrantha* (Junegrass). Dry soils.

If the florets disarticulate below the glumes, it is *Sphenopholis* (wedgegrass). See page 154.

Koeleria macrantha

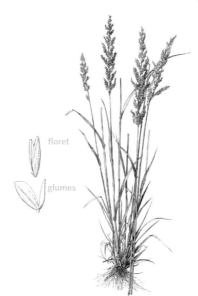

floret

glumes

spikelet

Koeleria macrantha

Sphenopholis obtusata

If the lemmas are awned, go to

page 59

If the lemmas are awnless, go to

page 56

If the spikelets occur on one side of the rachis, it is *Leptochloa* (sprangletop). See page 128.

If the spikelets occur on both sides of the rachis, it is *Melica* (melic). See page 129.

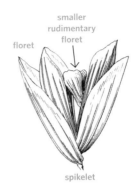

floret

smaller rudimentary floret

spikelet

Melica mutica

If the awn of the upper lemma is straight and the awn of the lower lemma is bent, it is *Arrhenatherum elatius*† (tall oatgrass). Tall grass of roadsides, fields, waste ground, wooded slopes; FACU.

If the awn of the upper lemma is bent and the awn of the lower lemma is straight, or if the awns of both lemmas are both bent or both straight, go to

below

Arrhenatherum elatius

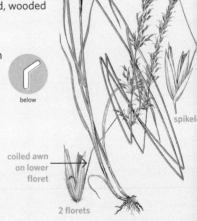

coiled awn on lower floret

2 florets

spikel●

Arrhenatherum elatius

If the spikelets disarticulate below the glumes, it is *Sphenopholis* (wedgegrass). See page 154.

If the spikelets disarticulate above the glumes, go to

page 57

If the lemma is membranous and the rachilla is prolonged behind the palea of the upper lemma, go to

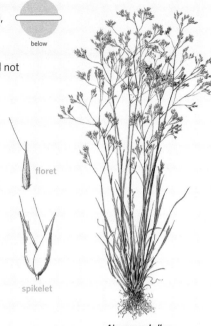

below

If the lemma is firm and the rachilla is short and not prolonged, it is *Aira*† (hairgrass). See page 81.

floret

spikelet

Aira caryophyllea

If the awns of the lemmas are attached above the middle, it is *Trisetum spicatum* (spike trisetum). Alpine meadows, shores.

If the awns of the lemmas are attached below the middle, it is *Deschampsia* (hairgrass). See page 101.

Trisetum spicatum

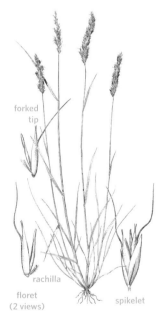

forked tip

rachilla

floret (2 views)

spikelet

Trisetum spicatum

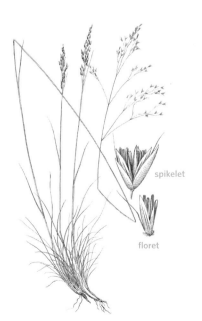

spikelet

floret

Deschampsia flexuosa

If the sheaths are velvety soft, it is *Holcus*† (velvetgrass). See page 125.

If the sheaths are smooth or hairy, but not velvety, go to

below

hooked awn on upper ♂ floret

floret pair

spikelet

Holcus lanatus

If the awn of the lemma is straight, it is *Sphenopholis* (wedgegrass). See page 154.

If the awn of the lemma is bent, go to

below

If the spikelets disarticulate below the glumes, it is *Sphenopholis* (wedgegrass). See page 154.

If the spikelets disarticulate above the glumes and . . .

the grass is tall (0.5–2 m), it is *Arrhenatherum elatius*† (tall oatgrass). See page 56.

the grass is short (< 0.5 m), it is *Aira*† (hairgrass). See page 81.

forked tip

awn

florets

spikelet

Aira elegans

If the lemmas are forked at the top (two teeth), go to

below

If the lemmas are not forked at top, go to

below

 If the awn is coiled and arises from the top of the lemma between the two teeth, it is *Danthonia* (oatgrass). See page 100.

If the awn is straight or bent and arises from the middle of the back of the lemma, it is *Tristeum spicatum* (spike trisetum). See page 57.

coiled awn

floret

spikelet

Danthonia spicata

 If the lemmas are minutely bearded and the rachilla is hairy, it is *Trisetum spicatum* (spike trisetum). See page 57.

If the lemma and rachilla are smooth to scabrous, it is *Sphenopholis* (wedgegrass). See page 154.

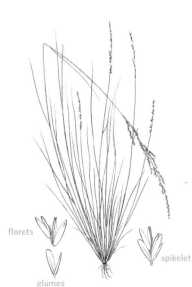

florets

glumes

spikelet

Sphenopholis filiformis

floret

glumes

Sphenopholis obtusata

from page 27

If there are mostly two or more spikelets side by side at each node, go to

below

If there is mostly one spikelet per node, go to

page 61

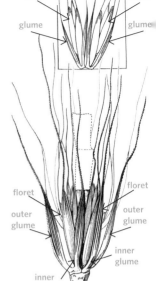

2 spikelets side by side

floret · floret

glume · glume

floret · floret

outer glume · outer glume

inner glume

inner glume

Elymus

2 spikelets side by side per node

one spikelet per node

Elymus

If there are mostly two spikelets side by side at each node, it is *Elymus* (wildrye). See page 114.

If there are mostly three spikelets side by side at each node (this may be easiest to see if you remove the spikelets from the rachis), it is *Hordeum* [*Critesion*] (barley). See page 126.

Tip: *Elymus* species often have clawlike auricles that clasp the stem.

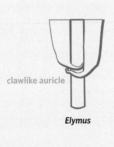

clawlike auricle

Elymus

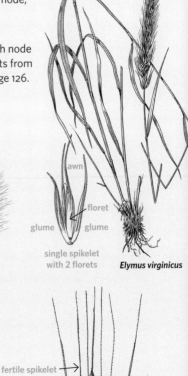

Hordeum jubatum. In noncultivated barley, the lateral spikelets are sterile and reduced in size, compared to the middle fertile spikelet.

fertile spikelet

sterile spikelet · sterile spikelet

Hordeum triad with three spikelets in a row

awn

floret

glume · glume

single spikelet with 2 florets

Elymus virginicus

If the spike is one-sided—that is, spikes are inserted in two rows on one or two sides (if the rachis is
triangular) of an elongate rachis—go to

below

If the spike is balanced, with spikelets inserted on
both sides of the rachis, go to

below

If the second glume bears a spine on the keel, it is *Ctenium
aromaticum* (toothache grass). Wet pine barrens on the
coastal plain; FACW.

If the second glume is spineless, go to

page 62

Ctenium aromaticum

one-sided
inflorescence

spine

spikelet

Ctenium aromaticum

If the spikelets are closely crowded and spread outward
from the rachis ± like tines on a two-sided comb, it is *Agropyron cristatum*† (crested wheatgrass). Disturbed areas.

If the spikelets are not so crowded and more
ascending to ± appressed to the rachis, go to

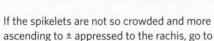

page 62

Agropyron cristatum

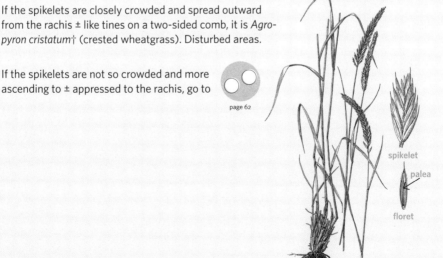

spikelet

palea

floret

Agropyron cristatum

If the grass is a tufted low annual of disturbed habitats, it is
Sclerochloa dura† (hardgrass). See page 50.

If the grass is a rhizomatous perennial of tidal marshes
and other alkaline habitats, it is *Spartina* (cordgrass). See
page 153.

rhizome

Spartina patens

If the spikelets are placed edgewise to the rachis, as shown,
it is *Lolium*† (ryegrass). See page 128.

If the spikelets are placed flat against the rachis, as shown,
it is *Elymus* (wildrye). See page 114.

Tip: In *Lolium*, because of the
placement of the spikelets
against the rachis, only the
topmost spikelet has both
glumes; all the other spikelets only have the glume
opposite the rachis.

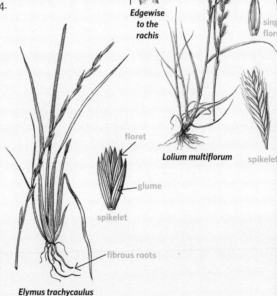

**Edgewise
to the
rachis**

singl
flore

floret

glume

spikelet

Lolium multiflorum

spikelet

**Flatwise to
the rachis**

fibrous roots

Elymus trachycaulus

from page 27

If the leaves are ± heart-shaped and clasp the stem and
the plant is decumbent, it is *Arthraxon hispidus*† (jointhead,
small carpetgrass). Moist meadows, waste ground.

If the leaves are linear (like a typical grass leaf),
go to

page 63

heart-
shaped
leaf

Arthraxon hispidus

If the rachis is triangular in cross section or winged, go to

below

If the rachis is not triangular or winged, go to

below

If the spikelets disarticulate above the glumes, go to

page 64

If the spikelets disarticulate below the glumes, it is *Digitaria* (crabgrass). See page 111.

fertile floret

winged rachis

spikelet

Digitaria ischaemum

If the plants are large (> 1 m tall), go to

page 64

If the plants are smaller (< 1 m tall), go to

page 64

If there is a single fertile floret per spikelet (there may be reduced or sterile florets present), go to

page 65

If there are three to six fertile florets per spikelet, it is *Eleusine indica*† (goosegrass). Lawns, gardens, disturbed areas; FACU.

Eleusine indica

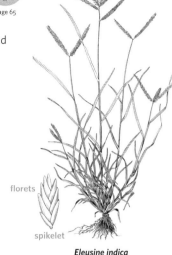

florets

spikelet

Eleusine indica

If the inflorescence is covered with silky hairs (either silvery to grayish or tawny to purplish) that extend past the spikelets, thus somewhat concealing them, it is *Miscanthus sinensis*† (eulalia). See page 22.

If the inflorescence is not covered in long silky hairs (the spikelet, rachis, and pedicels may be hairy), it is *Andropogon* (bluestem). See page 84.

If the ligule is membranous and there are three to six florets per spikelet, it is *Eleusine indica*† (goosegrass). Lawns, gardens, disturbed areas; FACU (regionwide). See above.

If the ligule is a ring of hairs and there is one floret per spikelet, it is *Cynodon dactylon*† (bermudagrass). Lawns, gardens, roadsides, pastures, fields, disturbed areas; FACU.

Cynodon dactylon

spikelet

floret

Cynodon dactylon

If the inflorescence branches are whorled, it is *Chloris verticillata*† (tumble windmill-grass). Native to midwestern United States; disturbed areas, bottomlands, fields.

If the inflorescence branches are not whorled, it is *Gymnopogon* (skeletongrass). See page 125.

Chloris verticillata

florets

Chloris verticillata

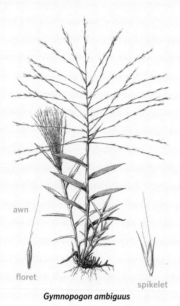

awn

floret

spikelet

Gymnopogon ambiguus

from page 21

If the inflorescence is ± one-sided (spikelets are attached on one side of the rachis), go to

page 66

If the spikelets are on both sides of the rachis, go to

page 66

If the plant is an erect tufted annual or perennial, it is *Cynosurus*† (dogtail). See page 100.

If the plant is a prostrate, matted annual, it is *Sclerochloa dura*† (hardgrass). See page 50.

Tip: In *Cynosurus*, the spike-lets are dimorphic—one is fertile, the other sterile. The spikelets are arranged on one side of the rachis, with the sterile spikelets concealing the fertile ones.

sterile spikelet

fertile spikelet

Cynosurus cristatus

awn

floret

Cynosurus echinatus

If the spikelets have long, stiff bristles, silky hairs, or awns that extend beyond and somewhat conceal the spikelets, giving the inflorescence a fuzzy look, go to

page 67

If the spikelets are not concealed by long bristles, silky hairs, or awns (the glumes and/or lemmas themselves may be hairy), go to

page 67

Setaria

Andropogon glomeratus

If the spikelets are paired at each node with one sessile and one pedicellate spikelet (the spikelet arrangement is a rame; in these grasses, the hairs of the spikelets and pedicels give the inflorescence its fuzzy appearance), go to

page 24

If the spikelets are solitary at each node, go to

below

If the glumes are fused, go to

page 68

If the glumes are free (not fused), go to

page 68

floret
awn
glumes
fully fused

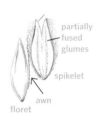

partially fused glumes

spikelet

awn
floret

If the glumes are awned (the awns of the glumes give the inflorescence its fuzzy appearance), it is *Polypogon monspeliensis*† (rabbitsfoot grass). Brackish marshes, disturbed areas; FACW.

If the glumes are awnless (the bristles beneath the spikelet give the inflorescence its fuzzy appearance), go to

page 68

Polypogon monspeliensis

floret

awn

glumes

Polypogon monspeliensis

If the glumes are fused together along their entire length and awned, it is *Phleum pratense*† (timothy). Cultivated and escaped to fields, meadows, and roadsides; FACU.

Phleum pratense

If the glumes are fused together only at the bottom and are not awned, it is *Alopecurus* (foxtail). See page 82.

Phleum pratense

Alopecurus

If the glumes are hairy, it is *Anthoxanthum* (vernalgrass). See page 85.

If the glumes are smooth or scabrous, go to

page 69 top

If the bristles fall with the spikelets when mature, it is *Pennisetum alopecuroides*† (foxtail fountaingrass). Disturbed areas.

If the bristles remain on the plant when mature, it is *Setaria* (foxtail grass, bristlegrass). See page 150.

Pennisetum alopecuroides

Tip: Bristles are not the same as awns. Bristles arise from the base of the spikelet or the sterile pedicels; awns arise from the glumes or lemmas and are extensions of the vascular tissues.

sterile bristles

spikelet

Setaria

If any part of the fertile lemma(s) is hairy, go to

below

If the fertile lemma(s) are smooth or scabrous, go to

below

If the entire lemma is hairy, or hairy at least on the veins and margins, and . . .

> there are paired sterile lemmas underlying the single fertile floret, it is *Phalaris* (canarygrass). See page 142.

> there are no sterile lemmas present and the fertile lemma is veinless or one-veined, it is *Sporobolus* (dropseed). See page 155.

> there are no sterile lemmas present and the fertile lemma is three-veined, it is *Muhlenbergia* (muhly). See page 130.

If the lemma is only hairy at the base (hairs may be long or short), go to

page 70

floret

glumes

Sporobolus vaginiflorus

If the spikelet has one fertile floret, go to

page 70

If the spikelet has two or more fertile florets, go to

page 70

If the hairs arise from the base of the lemma and are long (one-half the length to > the length of the lemma), stiff, and white, it is *Calamagrostis* (reedgrass). See page 96.

If the hairs are < one-half the length of the lemma (minutely bearded), go to

page 71

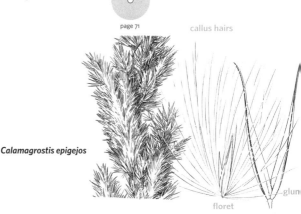

callus hairs

Calamagrostis epigejos

glume

floret

If the fertile floret is hard, smooth, shiny, and subtended (underlain) by two sterile, hairy lemmas, it is *Anthoxanthum* (vernalgrass; sterile lemmas are awned). See page 85.

If the fertile floret is leathery and the scalelike second glume has a sacklike base, it is *Sacciolepis striata* (American cupscale). Marshes, interdune swales, ditches, swamps; OBL.

Sacciolepis striata

If the fertile floret is membranous, go to

page 71

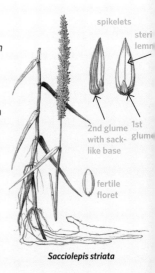

spikelets

sterile lemma

2nd glume with sacklike base

1st glume

fertile floret

Sacciolepis striata

If the spikelets are two-flowered, go to

page 72

If the spikelets are three- to many-flowered, it is *Glyceria* (mannagrass). See page 123.

palea

lemma

floret

Glyceria obtusa

If there is one floret per pair of glumes and . . .

the lemma is awnless, it is *Ammophila breviligulata* (American beachgrass). Dunes, beaches; UPL/FACU.

Ammophila breviligulata

the lemma has three awns, it is *Aristida* (threeawn). See page 87.

If there are two or more florets per pair of glumes, it is *Trisetum spicatum* (spike trisetum). See page 57.

Ammophila breviligulata

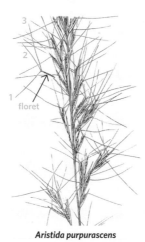

3
2
1
floret

Aristida purpurascens

floret   spikelet

If the inflorescence is cylindrical, and the plant is a prostrate annual, it is *Crypsis schoenoides*† (swamp pricklegrass). Disturbed areas; FACU.

Crypsis schoenoides

If the inflorescence is asymmetrical, lobed, or irregular, go to

page 72

spikelet   floret   glumes

Crypsis schoenoides

If the rachilla is very short and not prolonged behind the palea, it is *Aira*† (hairgrass). See page 81.

If the rachilla is prolonged behind the palea, it is *Trisetum spicatum* (spike trisetum). See page 57.

If the lemma has three awns, it is *Aristida* (threeawn). See page 87.

If the lemma is awnless, it is *Sporobolus* (dropseed). See page 155.

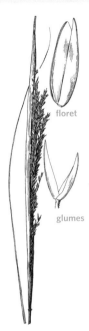

floret

glumes

Sporobolus compositus

from page 31

If the spikelets are somewhat concealed by sterile bristles, giving the inflorescence a fuzzy look, go to

page 73

If there are no sterile bristles or hairs underlying the spikelets, go to

page 73

If the inflorescence is a dense, cylindrical, spikelike panicle, go to

page 68

If the inflorescence is a raceme, it is *Echinochloa* (barnyard grass; some spp. with papillate-based hairs). See page 112.

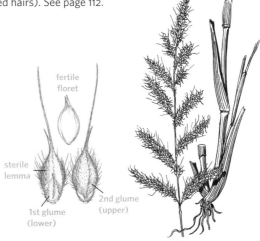

fertile floret

sterile lemma

1st glume (lower)

2nd glume (upper)

Echinochloa crus-galli

If the spikelets are arranged on one side of the rachis, as shown, go to

below

Raceme with spikelets on one side of the rachis

If the spikelets are arranged on both sides of the rachis, as shown, go to

page 74

Panicle

If the spikelets have a cuplike structure at the base, it is *Eriochloa villosa*† (Chinese cupgrass). Fields, meadows, and other disturbed areas.

If the spikelets do not have a cuplike structure at the base, go to

page 74

Eriochloa villosa

one-sided

cuplike structure

Eriochloa villosa

If the glumes, sterile lemma, or both are awned or awn-tipped, it is *Echinochloa* (barnyard grass). See page 112.

If the glumes and/or lemmas are awnless (may be long-pointed), go to

below

 If the fertile floret is hard, go to

page 75
(first couplet)

If the fertile floret is leathery, it is *Digitaria* (crabgrass). See page 111.

 If the fertile floret is leathery, go to

page 75
(second couplet)

If the fertile floret is hard and the surface is smooth, go to

page 76

If the first glume is present, go to

page 76

If the first glume is absent, it is *Paspalum* (paspalum).
See page 139.

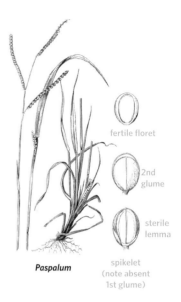

fertile floret

2nd glume

sterile lemma

Paspalum

spikelet
(note absent
1st glume)

 If the second glume has an expanded, sacklike base, it is
Sacciolepis striata (American cupscale). See page 70.

If the second glume does not have an expanded base, it is
Digitaria cognata [*Leptoloma cognatum*] (fall witchgrass).
See page 111.

If the second glume and sterile lemma are narrow and typically taper to a long, sharp tip, it is *Panicum* (panicgrass). See page 135.

Note: Two *Dichanthelium* species have ± pointy spikelets: *D. depauperatum*, in which the second glume and sterile lemma are prolonged into a beak, and *D. scabriusculum*, a coastal plant that often has a band of glandular tissue below each node and sheaths that are mottled or white striped.

If the second glume and sterile lemma are oval to round and bluntly pointed or rounded at the tip, it is *Dichanthelium* (panicgrass). See page 102.

Note: *Panicum verrucosum* has bluntish spikelets, but they are covered with warty bumps.

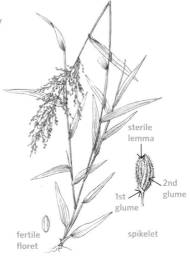

fertile floret

sterile lemma

1st glume

2nd glume

spikelet

Panicum virgatum

sterile lemma

1st glume

2nd glume

fertile floret

spikelet

Dichanthelium annulum

If the surface of the fertile lemma is strongly wrinkled and warty, it is *Urochloa* [*Brachiaria*] (signalgrass, millet). See page 157.

If the surface of the fertile lemma is smooth, it is *Echinochloa* (barnyard grass). See page 112.

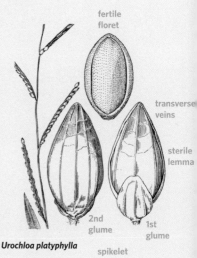

fertile floret

transverse veins

sterile lemma

2nd glume

1st glume

Urochloa platyphylla

spikelet

Genera Keys

**The following keys apply to
genera with multiple species.**

Agrostis (bentgrass)

Tip: The florets of *Agrostis* are papery and translucent.

If the palea is one-half as long as the lemma or longer (the palea should be readily visible), go to

If the palea is < one-quarter as long as the lemma, or is absent, go to

If the spikelets are sparse and located toward the tips of the branches, and the leaf blades are ≤ 4 mm wide, it is *A. capillaris*† (Rhode Island bent). Meadows, roadsides, disturbed areas; (FAC).

Agrostis capillaris

If the spikelets are crowded along the panicle branches, the leaf blades are mostly > 4 mm wide, and . . .

Agrostis gigantea

    the panicle is open, usually red-purple, and the plant is erect and rhizomatous, it is *A. gigantea*† (redtop). Fields, roadsides, disturbed areas; (FACW).

    the panicle is contracted, yellow-brown, and the plant is often decumbent and not rhizomatous, it is *A. stolonifera*† (creeping bent). Wet, moist, or dry disturbed areas.

Agrostis stolonifera

A. gigantea

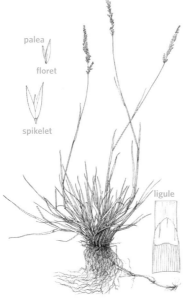

A. stolonifera

A. capillaris

C If the plant is an annual and the lemma has two minute setae (hairs) at the tip and usually a long awn (to 10 mm), it is *A. elliottiana* (Elliott's bent). Dry, open soils, rock outcrops; facultative upland (FACU).

If the plant is a perennial and is awned or awnless, go to **D**

Agrostis elliottiana

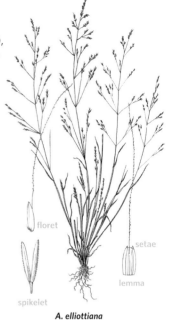

floret

setae

spikelet

lemma

A. elliottiana

D If the awn of the lemma is bent, go to **E**

If the awn of the lemma is absent or ± straight, go to **F**

E If the panicle branches are scabrous, it is *A. canina†* (velvet bent). Roadsides, open areas, lawns; FACU.

If the panicle branches are ± smooth, it is *A. mertensii* (northern bent). Thin soils in high elevations, rocky summits; FACU.

Agrostis canina

Agrostis mertensii

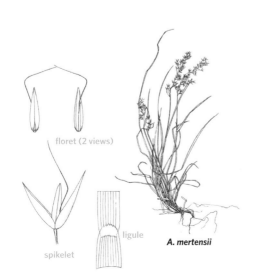

floret (2 views)

ligule

spikelet

A. mertensii

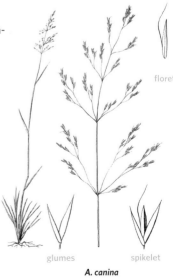

floret

glumes

spikelet

A. canina

If the leaf blades are often rolled inward (involute), and the panicle branches fork well above the middle and are ± tinged red, go to

Agrostis perennans

If the leaf blades are flat, and the panicle branches fork near or below the middle and are pale (seldom tinged red), it is *A. perennans* (autumn bent). Woodlands, forests, roadsides; FACU.

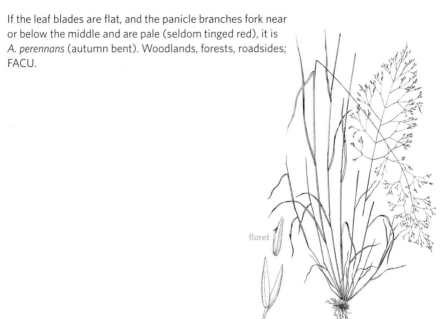

floret

glumes

A. perennans

If the spikelets are borne on short pedicels (0.3–2 mm long), thus appearing clustered, it is *A. hyemalis* (winter bent). Blooms early, May–June. Roadsides and other disturbed habitats; FAC.

Agrostis hyemalis

If the spikelets are borne on long pedicels (0.5–5 mm long), thus not appearing clustered, it is *A. scabra* (ticklegrass). Blooms later, July–September. Moist, sandy-peaty grounds, barrens; FAC.

Agrostis scabra

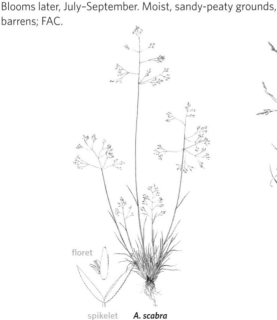

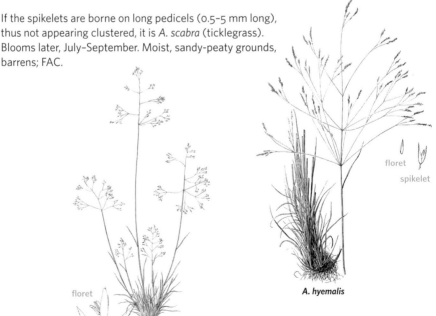

floret
spikelet

A. hyemalis

floret

spikelet   **A. scabra**

Aira (hairgrass)

If the inflorescence is spikelike, it is *A. praecox*† (spike hairgrass). Fields, roadsides, disturbed areas.

Aira praecox

If the inflorescence is open and diffuse, go to B

floret

spikelet

A. praecox

If the spikelet pedicels are short (one to two times as long as the spikelets) and both lemmas are awned, it is *A. caryophyllea*† (silver hairgrass). Fields, roadsides, disturbed areas mostly near the coast; FAC.

Aira caryophyllea

If the spikelet pedicels are longer (two to five times as long as the spikelets) and the lower lemma is often awnless, it is *A. elegans*† (hairgrass). Fields, roadsides, disturbed areas.

Aira elegans

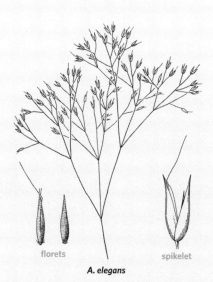

florets

spikelet

A. elegans

floret

spikelet

A. caryophyllea

Alopecurus (foxtail)

If the glumes are blunt at the tip with ± irregular teeth, go to

If the tips of the glumes are pointed and have winged margins, go to

If the awn is ± equal to the glumes in length or surpasses them by < 1 mm, it is *A. aequalis* (shortawn foxtail). Wet swales, wet meadows, ditches, shores; FACW.

Alopecurus aequalis

If the awn is > the glumes in length by at least 1.5 mm, go to

floret

fused glumes

A. aequalis

If the keels of the glumes are hairy (especially above the middle), it is *A. pratensis*† (meadow foxtail). Roadsides, fields; FAC/FACW.

Alopecurus pratensis

If the keels of the glumes are hairy below the middle but scabrous above, it is *A. myosuroides*† (slender meadow foxtail). Moist fields.

Alopecurus myosuroides

floret

fused glumes

A. myosuroides

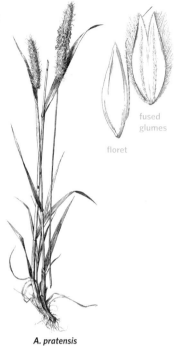

fused glumes

floret

A. pratensis

If the plant is a perennial and the inflorescence is often tinged purple, it is *A. geniculatus*† (water foxtail). Disturbed areas; obligate wetland (OBL).

lopecurus geniculatus

If the plant is a densely tufted annual and the inflorescence is not purple-tinged, it is *A. carolinianus* (tufted foxtail). Moist fields, ditches, forests; FACW.

Alopecurus carolinianus

floret

fused glumes

A. carolinianus

floret

floret

fused glumes

A. geniculatus

Andropogon (bluestem)

If the inflorescence is a ± digitate cluster of mostly three to four racemes, resembling a turkey's foot, it is *A. gerardii* (big bluestem). Wide variety of habitats; FAC.

Andropogon gerardii

If the inflorescence is compact and bushy and the upper leaves are spathelike, enclosing the peduncle and the base of the racemes (glomerule), it is *A. glomeratus* (bushy bluestem). Swamps, wet savannahs, pine flatwoods, wet disturbed sites; FACW.

Andropogon glomeratus

If the inflorescence is slender and elongate and comprises paired racemes, go to

B

spikelet

A. gerardii

spikelet

A. glomeratus

glomerule of spikelets

B

If the sessile spikelet of the rame is longer than its paired sterile pedicel, and the leaves are purplish-glaucous, it is *A. ternarius* (split bluestem). Open woods, dry fields.

Andropogon ternarius

If the sessile spikelet of the rame is shorter than its paired sterile pedicel, and the leaves are brownish to coppery, go to

C

paired racemes

spikelet **A. ternarius**

C

If the fertile spikelet has a straight awn, it is *A. virginicus* (broomsedge). Old fields, hillsides, disturbed sites; FAC/FACU.

If the awn of the fertile spikelet is loosely twisted at the base, it is *A. gyrans* (Elliott's beardgrass). Dry or moist fields, open woods; FAC/OBL.

Andropogon virginicus

Andropogon gyrans

paired racemes

spikelet

A. virginicus

spikelet

A. gyrans

Anthoxanthum (vernalgrass)

A

If the sterile lemmas are long-awned (awns > 2 mm), go to **B**

If the sterile lemmas are awnless or short-awned (awns to 1 mm), go to **C**

B

If the plants are erect with unbranching stems, and the awn of the lower sterile lemma is straight, it is *A. odoratum*† (sweet vernalgrass). Lawns, roadsides, disturbed areas; common; FACU.

Anthoxanthum
odoratum

If the plants are low-growing with branching stems, and both sterile lemmas have bent awns, it is *A. aristatum*† (vernalgrass). Roadsides, disturbed areas.

Anthoxanthum
aristatum

spikelet
(side
view)

A. aristatum

A. odoratum

sterile
lemmas

fertile
floret

spikelet
(side
view)

C

If the hairs at the tip of the fertile floret are < 0.5 mm long, with longer hairs concentrated near the midvein, and the plant is coastal, it is *A. nitens*† [*Hierochloe odorata*] (vanilla sweetgrass). Saltmarsh edges.

Anthoxanthum nitens

If the hairs at the tip of the fertile floret are 0.5–1 mm long and evenly distributed, and the plant is inland, it is *A. hirtum* [*Hierochloe odorata*] (vanilla sweetgrass). Fens, wet calcareous meadows.

Anthoxanthum hirtum

sterile
lemmas

fertile
floret

spikelet

A. nitens

Aristida (threeawn)

A If the central awn is longer than the two lateral awns, go to

If all three awns are ± equal in length, go to

B If the central awn, when dry, is loosely spirally coiled at the base, it is *A. dichotoma* (churchmouse threeawn). Roadsides, fields, disturbed areas; FACU/UPL.

If the central awn, when dry, is bent or reflexed but not coiled, go to

Aristida dichotoma

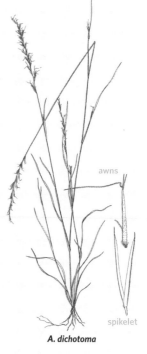

awns

spikelet

A. dichotoma

C If the plant is a perennial, it is *A. purpurascens* (arrowfeather threeawn). Dry sandy soils; FACW/FAC.

If the plant is an annual, go to

Aristida purpurascens

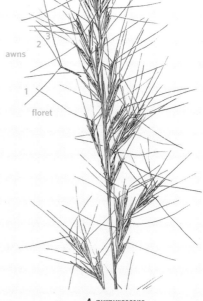

awns
3
2
1
floret

A. purpurascens

D If the leaf sheaths are woolly, it is *A. lanosa* (woolly three-awn). Dry sandy soils, chiefly in the coastal plain.

If the leaf sheaths are smooth to hairy, but not woolly, go to **F**

Aristida lanosa

A. lanosa   woolly sheath

E If the awns are deciduous and twisted together at the base into a column, it is *A. tuberculosa* (seaside threeawn). Coastal dunes and other dry sandy habitats in the coastal plain.

If the awns are persistent and free at the base, it is *A. oligantha* (oldfield threeawn). Roadsides, fields, disturbed areas.

Aristida tuberculosa

Aristida oligantha

column

A. tuberculosa

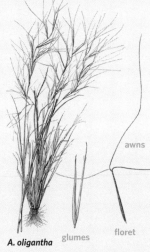

awns

A. oligantha   glumes   floret

F If the plant is an annual, it is *A. longespica* (slimspike three-awn). Disturbed areas; FACU/UPL.

If the plant is a perennial, it is *A. purpurascens* (arrowfeather threeawn). See page 87.

Aristida longispica

A. longispica

Avena (oat)

Avena sativa

Avena fatua

A. sativa† (oat). Lemmas smooth or scabrous, but not hairy; awn, if present, straight and only on first (lower) lemma. Fields, disturbed areas; common; UPL.

A. fatua† (wild oat). Lemmas with white or brown hairs; first two with well-developed awns that are bent and twisted at the base. Disturbed areas.

floret

A. sativa

floret

spikelet

A. fatua

Brachyelytrum (shorthusk)

Brachyelytrum erectum

Brachyelytrum aristosum

B. erectum (southern shorthusk, long-awned wood grass). Lemma hairy on the veins, with hairs > 0.3 mm long; mid-vein distinct. Mesic forests; FACU.

B. aristosum (northern shorthusk). Lemma scabrous due to short hairs, which are < 0.3 mm long; midvein not distinct. Moist forests at moderate to high elevations.

floret glumes

B. erectum

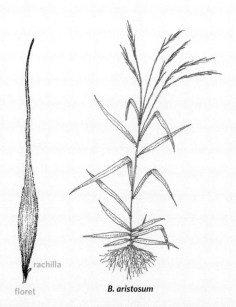

rachilla

floret

B. aristosum

89

Briza (quakinggrass)

Briza media

Briza minor

B. media † (perennial quakinggrass). Perennial with a truncate ligule, about 1 mm long. Disturbed areas; FACU/UPL.

B. minor † (lesser quakinggrass). Annual with an elongate ligule, ≥ 3 mm long. Fields, disturbed areas; common; FAC/FACW.

B. media

spikelet

B. minor

Bromus (brome)

A

Tip: In *Bromus*, the lemmas have two teeth at their tip, and the awn is between the teeth.

Tip: The lemma resembles a dugout canoe when flipped on its back, and the palea often has a fringe of hairs along the margin.

Bromus tectorum

Bromus sterilis

If the lemmas are long and slender, 8–18 mm long (not including the awn) by 0.8–1.5 mm wide (side view), ending in two long, slender, pointed teeth, and . . .

the awns of the lemmas are 1–2 cm long and the palea is shorter than the lemma, it is *B. tectorum*† (cheatgrass). Disturbed areas.

the awns of the lemmas are 2–3 cm long and the palea almost equals the lemma in length, it is *B. sterilis*† (barren brome). Disturbed areas.

palea

long teeth

floret

spikelet

B. tectorum

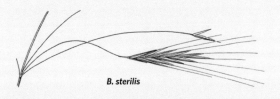

B. sterilis

Bromus squarrosus

If the lemmas are very broad, 2.5–3.5 mm wide (side view) by 8–11 mm long (not including the awn), it is *B. squarrosus*† (squarrose brome). Introduced in waste places.

If the lemmas are neither very slender nor very broad (see measurements above), go to

B. squarrosus

Bromus catharticus

If the lemmas are sharply keeled (folded), it is *B. catharticus*† [*B. willdenowii*] (rescue grass). Disturbed areas.

If the lemmas are rounded to only slightly keeled, go to

B. catharticus

If the second (upper) glume has five to nine veins, go to

If the second glume has three veins, go to

If the plant is a perennial and the awn is equal to or shorter than the body of the lemma, go to

If the plant is an annual and the awn is variable in length with respect to the body of the lemma, go to

If the plant has creeping rhizomes with dark brown scales (often becoming colonial), it is *B. inermis*† (smooth brome). Cultivated and escaped to fields, roadsides, and disturbed areas; UPL.

Bromus inermis

If the plant does not have rhizomes (often tufted), go to

B. inermis

spikelet

floret
(2 views)

If the awns of the lemmas are 2–3 mm long, there are 3-6 leaves/stem, and the stem nodes are exposed, it is *B. kalmii* (Kalm's brome). Forests and woodlands, barrens, ridgetop oak forests; FACU.

Bromus kalmii

If the awns of the lemmas are 5–8 mm long, there are 6-8 leaves/stem, and the stem nodes are covered by the sheaths, it is *B. nottowayanus* (Virginia brome). Moist forests along stream bottoms.

Bromus nottowayanus

floret

spikelet

B. nottowayanus

floret

B. kalmii

G

If the panicle is open with spreading to drooping branches, go to **I**

If the panicle branches are ± erect, go to **J**

 H

If the lemmas are smooth, it is *B. erectus*† (meadow brome). Disturbed areas.

If any part of the lemma is hairy, go to **K**

Bromus erectus

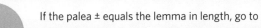

 I

If the palea ± equals the lemma in length, go to **L**

If the palea is shorter than the lemma, go to **M**

Bromus hordeaceus

J If the panicle is dense and compact, it is *B. hordeaceus*† (lopgrass). Disturbed areas; UPL.

If the panicle is more open, go to

floret

B. hordeaceus

K If the pedicels are stiff and erect and mostly shorter than the spikelets, it is *B. erectus*† (meadow brome). See page 93.

If the pedicels are often drooping and mostly longer than the spikelets, go to

floret

B. racemosus

L If the margins of the lemma overlap, concealing the rachilla, and . . .

the panicle is wide (up to 30 cm), it is *B. arvensis*† (field brome). Roadsides, fields, waste places; FACU.

the panicle is narrower (seldom over 15 cm), it is *B. racemosus*† (smooth brome). Disturbed areas.

Bromus arvensis

If the margins of the lemma are curled under, exposing the rachilla, it is *B. secalinus*† (ryebrome). Disturbed areas.

floret

Bromus racemosus

Bromus secalinus

B. arvensis

rachilla concealed

B. secalinus

note exposed rachilla

spikelet

M

If the awns are wavy and flexuous, it is *B. japonicus*† (Japanese brome). Disturbed areas; FACU.

If the awns are straight and stiff, it is *B. commutatus*† (meadow brome). Disturbed areas.

Bromus japonicus

Bromus commutatus

spikelet

note divergent awns

floret

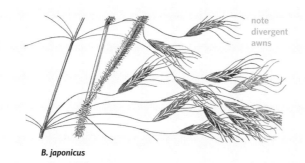

B. japonicus

B. commutatus

N

If the margins of the lemma are curled under, exposing the rachilla, it is *B. secalinus*† (ryebrome). See page 94.

If the margins of the lemma overlap, concealing the rachilla, and . . .

the panicle is wide (to 30 cm), it is *B. arvensis*† (field brome). See page 94.

the panicle is narrower (seldom over 15 cm), it is *B. racemosus*† (smooth brome). See page 94.

O

If the lemmas are hairy mainly along the margins, it is *B. ciliatus* (fringed brome). Moist woods and other wet places at high elevations; FACW.

If the lemmas are hairy throughout, go to  **P**

Bromus ciliatus

floret

spikelet

B. ciliatus

P If the stems have eight to twenty leaves, and the upper stem nodes are concealed by the sheaths, it is *B. latiglumis* [*B. altissimus*] (hairy woodbrome). Alluvial soils along rivers; FACW.

If the stems have four to six leaves, and the upper stem nodes are exposed, it is *B. pubescens* (Canada brome). Rich moist woods on rocky slopes; FACU.

Bromus latiglumis

Bromus pubescens

spikelet   floret

B. pubescens

Calamagrostis (reedgrass)

A If the callus hairs greatly exceed the lemma in length, it is *C. epigejos*† (feathertop). Disturbed woods, roadsides, waste ground.

If the callus hairs are shorter than or as long as the lemma, go to **B**

Calamagrostis epigejos

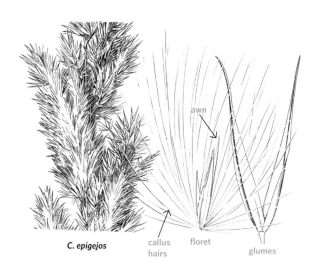

C. epigejos   callus hairs   floret   awn   glumes

B

If the awn is distinctly bent and twisted, it is *C. porteri* (Porter's reedgrass). Dry to moist forests.

If the awn is not bent or twisted, go to **C**

Calamagrostis porteri

callus hairs

spikelet

C. porteri

C

If the awn is inserted near the lemma tip, it is *C. cinnoides* [*C. coarctata*] (Nuttall's reedgrass). Swamps, wet woods.

If the awn is inserted near the middle of the lemma, go to **D**

Calamagrostis cinnoides

floret

glumes

C. cinnoides

D

If the inflorescence is dense and erect, it is *C. stricta* (slim-stem reedgrass). Moist meadows, calcareous wetlands; FACW.

If the inflorescence is open and lax, it is *C. canadensis* (Canada bluejoint). Wet meadows, bogs, swamps; OBL/FACW.

Calamagrostis stricta

Calamagrostis canadensis

awn

C. canadensis

spikelet

awn

glumes

floret

C. stricta

Calamovilfa (sandreed)

Calamovilfa brevipilis

Calamovilfa longifolia

C. brevipilis (pine-barren sandreed). Lemma and palea hairy, in addition to callus hairs. Swamps and bogs in the coastal plain; OBL.

C. longifolia (prairie sandreed). Lemma and palea smooth, except for callus hairs. Dry, sandy soils; inland.

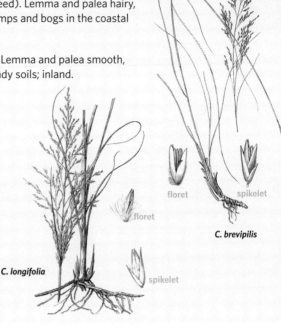

floret

spikelet

C. brevipilis

floret

C. longifolia

spikelet

Cenchrus (sandbur)

Cenchrus longispinus

A If the spines are slender and there are > forty spines per bur, it is *C. longispinus* (mat sandbur). Sandy soils, disturbed habitats; FACU/UPL.

If the spines are stout and fewer in number (< forty spines per bur), go to **B**

Cenchrus tribuloides

Cenchrus spinifex

B If the burs are densely long-haired and the spikelets are concealed within the burs, it is *C. tribuloides* (sanddune sandbur). Coastal sands, especially on dunes; FACU/UPL.

If the burs are short-haired or smooth, the spikelets are exerted at the tip of the bur, and the plant is southern, it is *C. spinifex* [*C. incertus*] (coastal sandbur). Sandy soils.

C. tribuloides

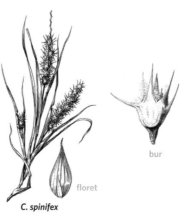

floret

bur

C. spinifex

bur

Chasmanthium (river oats, chasmanthium)

If the panicle has open, drooping branches, it is *C. latifolium* (river oats, broadleaf chasmanthium). Riverbanks, streambanks, bottomland forests; FAC/FACU.

If the panicle is strict with ascending branches, go to

Chasmanthium latifolium

spikelet   floret

C. latifolium

If the sheaths are essentially smooth except for long hairs on the margin, it is *C. laxum* (slender chasmanthium). Swamps, other moist habitats; common; FACW/FAC.

If the sheaths are hairy (at least at the summit), it is *C. sessiliflorum* (longleaf chasmanthium). Rich woods, meadows, swamps; FAC.

Chasmanthium laxum

Chasmanthium sessiliflorum

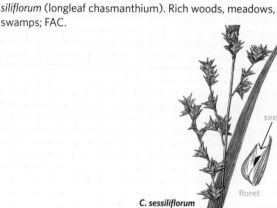

seed

floret

C. sessiliflorum

seed

floret

C. laxum

Cinna (woodreed)

Cinna arundinacea

C. arundinacea (stout woodreed). Inflorescence usually dense with ascending branches, second glume three-veined, awn usually < 0.5 mm long. Bottomland forests, rocky bars on rivers, other low, wet places; common; FACW.

Cinna latifolia

C. latifolia (drooping woodreed). Inflorescence open with spreading to drooping branches, second glume one-veined, awn to 1.5 mm long. Moist forests at high elevations; FACW.

minute awn

floret

glumes

C. arundinacea

minute awn

floret

glumes

C. latifolia

Cynosurus (dogtail grass)

Cynosurus echinatus

Cynosurus cristatus

C. echinatus† (bristly dogtail). Annual plant, inflorescence oval to round and dense, awns of lemmas 5–10 mm long. Lawns, roadsides.

C. cristatus† (crested dogtail). Perennial plant, inflorescence slender, awns of lemmas ≤ 1 mm long. Lawns, roadsides; UPL.

Tip: *Cynosurus* has dimorphic spikelets—one sterile and one fertile—that are paired and positioned on one side of the axis.

floret

C. echinatus

sterile spikelet   fertile spikelet

spiklelets

C. cristatus

Danthonia (oatgrass)

A

If the lemma teeth are broadly triangular, it is *D. spicata* (poverty oatgrass). Dry woodlands, rock outcrops, shale barrens.

Danthonia spicata

If the lemma teeth are slender and awnlike, go to   B

broadly triangular teeth

floret

spiklelets

D. spicata

B If the awn of the lemma is ≤ 10 mm long, it is *D. compressa* (flattened oatgrass). Rock outcrops, woodlands; FACU.

If the awn of the lemma is > 10 mm long, go to **C**

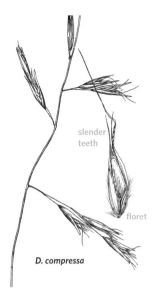

slender teeth

floret

D. compressa

Danthonia compressa

C If the sheaths are hairy and the awn of the lemma is coiled several times, it is *D. sericea* (downy oatgrass). Woodlands and dry, sandy soils in the coastal plain; FACU.

If the sheaths are smooth and the awn of the lemma is coiled once, it is *D. epilis* (bog oatgrass). Peaty bogs and seeps in the coastal plain; OBL.

Danthonia sericea

Danthonia epilis

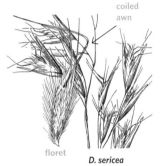

coiled awn

floret

D. sericea

Deschampsia (hairgrass)

Deschampsia cespitosa

Deschampsia flexuosa

D. cespitosa (tufted hairgrass). Lemmas smooth, awns ± straight, leaf blades flat or folded. Serpentine barrens, sandy shores, thickets; FACW.

D. flexuosa [*Avenella flexuosa*] (wavy hairgrass). Lemmas scabrous, awns strongly bent or twisted near the base, leaf blades very slender, curled inward. Dry woods, rocky slopes.

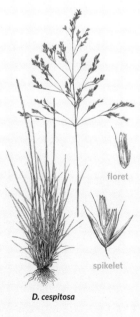

floret

spikelet

D. cespitosa

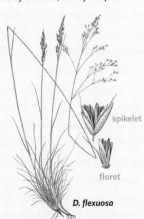

spikelet

floret

D. flexuosa

101

Diarrhena (beakgrain)

Diarrhena americana

Diarrhena obovata

D. americana (American beakgrain). Tips of lemmas pointed, bases ± hairy (bearded) except on first lemma. Rich woods.

D. obovata (obovate beakgrain). Tips of lemmas rounded, bases smooth. Alluvial forests, other moist forests; FAC/FACU.

bottle-shaped seed

bea
call

floret

spikelet

D. americana

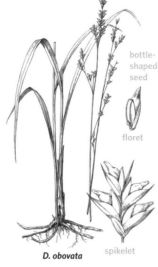

bottle-shaped seed

floret

spikelet

D. obovata

Dichanthelium (panicgrass)*

A

If the longest stem leaves are long and slender (fifteen to twenty times as long as they are wide), go to **B**

If the longest stem leaves are wider (generally < fifteen times as long as they are wide), go to **C**

B

If the tips of the second glume and sterile lemma are prolonged beyond the fruit into a beak extending 0.5–1.5 mm beyond the fertile lemma, it is *D. depauperatum* (starved panicgrass). Dry or sandy soils, open woods; common.

Dichanthelium
depauperatum

If the tips are not prolonged into a beak, go to **D**

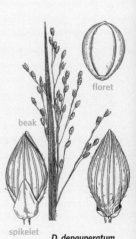

floret

beak

spikelet
(2 views)   *D. depauperatum*

C

If the hairs of the sheaths and stem are of two types (bistratal)—short soft hairs that intermingle with longer coarser hairs, which are appressed to spreading—it is *D. ovale* [*D. commonsianum*] (stiff-leaved panicgrass). Dry to damp sandy pinelands; FACU.

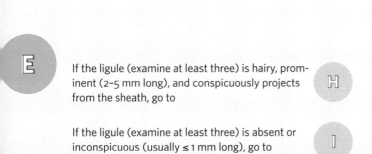
Dichanthelium ovale

If the hairs of the sheaths and stems are all alike, or if the sheaths and stems are smooth (not including the cilia along the margin), go to **E**

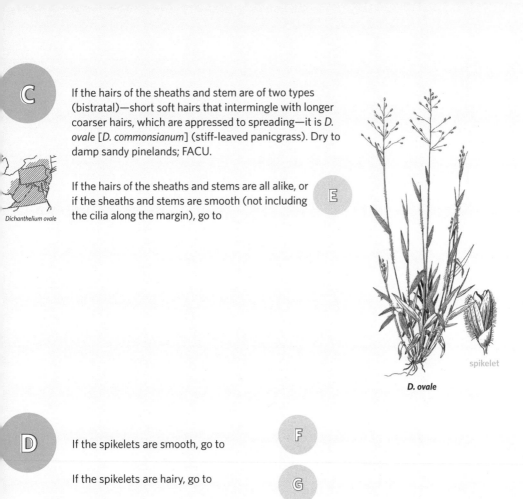
spikelet

D. ovale

D

If the spikelets are smooth, go to **F**

If the spikelets are hairy, go to **G**

E

If the ligule (examine at least three) is hairy, prominent (2–5 mm long), and conspicuously projects from the sheath, go to **H**

If the ligule (examine at least three) is absent or inconspicuous (usually ≤ 1 mm long), go to **I**

Dichanthelium strigosum

Dichanthelium linearifolium

F If the spikelets are ≤ 1.5 mm long, it is *D. strigosum* (cushion-tufted panicgrass). Sandy, low open pine woods, bogs; FAC.

If the spikelets are ≥ 1.7 mm long, it is *D. linearifolium* (linear-leaved panicgrass). Dry open woods; common.

spikelet
(2 views)

fertile
floret

D. linearifolium

spikelet
(2 views)

fertile
floret

D. strigosum

Dichanthelium aciculare

Dichanthelium laxiflorum

G If the spikelets are finely hairy, it is *D. aciculare* (narrow-leaved panicgrass). Rare in wet grasslands, prairielike barrens; FACU.

If the spikelets are soft-haired and the hairs are papillose at the base, it is *D. laxiflorum* (soft-tufted panicgrass). Woods; FAC/FACU.

If the spikelets are sparsely hairy, it is *D. linearifolium* (linear-leaved panicgrass). See above.

fertile
floret

fertile
floret

spikelet

spikelet

spike

D. aciculare

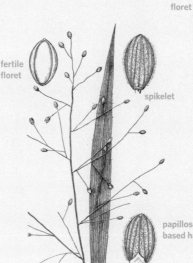

papillose-
based hairs

D. laxiflorum spikelet

H

If the spikelets are > 3 mm long, turgid and shiny, and sparsely pustulose-hairy (stems purplish and bearded at the nodes), it is *D. ravenelii* (Ravenel's panicgrass). Dry sandy or rocky soils of woods and clearings; FACU.

If the spikelets are 1–2 mm long, yellowish-green to olive to purple, and variously hairy, it is *D. acuminatum* (hairy panicgrass). Dry sandy and clayey soils of open woods and disturbed areas; FAC.

Dichanthelium ravenelii

Dichanthelium acuminatum

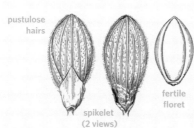

pustulose hairs

spikelet (2 views)

fertile floret

D. ravenelii

fertile floret (2 views)

spikelet (side view)

D. acuminatum

I

If the leaves are velvety (note viscid ring just below the nodes), it is *D. scoparium* (velvety panicgrass). Moist sandy soils of woodland openings and ditches; FACW.

If the leaves are smooth or ± hairy, but not velvety, go to **J**

Dichanthelium scoparium

viscid ring

spikelet

spikelet

D. scoparium

J

If the leaf blades are distinctly heart-shaped at the base, go to **K**

If the leaf blades are rounded to narrowed at the base, go to **L**

K If the spikelets are elliptical and mostly > 2 mm long, go to **M**

If the spikelets are round and mostly < 2 mm long, go to **N**

L If the second glume and sterile lemma noticeably exceed the fertile lemma in length, it is *D. scabriusculum* (tall swamp panicgrass). Wet, sandy soils of the coastal plain.

If the second glume and sterile lemma are shorter than, equal to, or barely exceed the fertile lemma in length, go to **O**

Dichanthelium scabriusculum

mottled sheath

spikelet (2 views)

fertile floret

D. scabriusculum

M If the primary leaf veins (including the midvein) are sharply differentiated from the secondary veins, and the spikelets are 2.5–5.2 mm long, go to **P**

If the primary and secondary leaf veins (excluding the midvein) are scarcely differentiated from each other, and the spikelets are 1.9–3.4 mm long, go to **Q**

N

If the panicle is narrow and the uppermost leaf blade (flag leaf) is ≥ 10 cm long, it is *D. polyanthes* (many-flowered panicgrass). Roadsides, open woods.

If the panicle is ovoid and the uppermost leaf blade (flag leaf) is < 10 cm long, it is *D. sphaerocarpon* (round-fruited panicgrass). Dry woods, thickets, old fields; FACU.

Dichanthelium
polyanthes

Dichanthelium
sphaerocarpon

fertile
floret
(2 views)

D. polyanthes

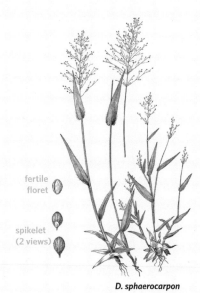

fertile
floret

spikelet
(2 views)

D. sphaerocarpon

O

If the spikelets are small (mostly 1–3 mm long, but up to 4 mm in *D. aciculare*), go to **R**

If the spikelets are larger (mostly 3–4 mm long), go to **S**

P

If the stems are densely bearded at the nodes, it is *D. boscii* (Bosc's panicgrass). Mesic to dry woods.

If the stems are ± smooth to short-haired on the nodes, go to **T**

Dichanthelium boscii

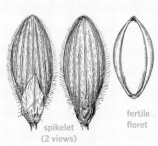

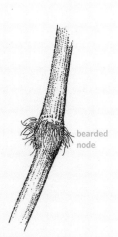

bearded
node

fertile
floret

spikelet
(2 views)

D. boscii

Q If the larger stem leaves are spreading and broadest near the base, it is *D. commutatum* (variable panicgrass). Rocky woods, thickets; FAC/FACU.

If the larger stem leaves are erect/ascending and broadest at or just below the middle, it is *D. boreale* (northern panicgrass). Open woods, thickets, wet meadows and fields; FACU.

Dichanthelium commutatum

Dichanthelium boreale

fertile floret (2 views)

spikelet (3 views)

D. boreale

veins scarcely differentiated

spikelet

spikelet

D. commutatum

R If the second glume and sterile lemma are about equal to the fertile lemma in length, it is *D. aciculare* (narrow-leaved panicgrass). See page 104.

If the second glume and sterile lemma are shorter than the fertile lemma, go to

S If the spikelets are papillose-hairy (hairs ≥ 0.5 mm), it is *D. leibergii* (Leiberg's panicgrass). Limestone outcrops.

If the spikelets are smooth or only minutely hairy, go to

Dichanthelium leibergii

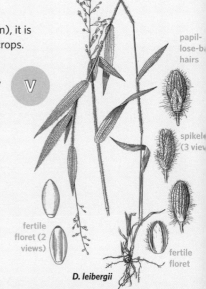

papil-lose-b hairs

spikele (3 view

fertile floret (2 views)

fertile floret

D. leibergii

T If the sheaths are smooth (not including the cilia along the margin) or covered with long, soft hairs, it is *D. latifolium* (broadleaved panicgrass). Open or shady forests; FACU.

If at least some sheaths are covered with short, stiff hairs arising from warty bumps (papillae), it is *D. clandestinum* (deer-tongue grass). Woodlands, ditches, low areas; FACW/FAC.

Dichanthelium latifolium

Dichanthelium clandestinum

spikelet (3 views)

papillose-hairy sheath

fertile floret

spikelet (2 views)

D. clandestinum

fertile floret (3 views)

D. latifolium

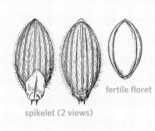

U If the leaf blades are 5–12 cm long, it is *D. dichotomum* (forked panicgrass). Widespread in wet to dry woods; FAC.

If the leaf blades are 1–5 cm long, and the plant is coastal, it is *D. ensifolium* (sword-leaf panicgrass). Wet to moist sandy pinelands, savannahs, bogs.

Dichanthelium dichotomum

Dichanthelium ensifolium

spikelet (2 views)

fertile floret

floret (2 views)

spikelet (2 views)

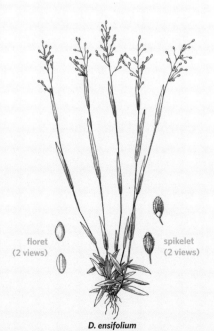

D. ensifolium

D. dichotomum

If the panicle is narrow with erect branches, it is *D. xantho-physum* (pale panicgrass). Dry, rocky slopes or sandy, open woods; mostly in the mountains.

If the panicle is ovoid with spreading or ascending branch-es, it is *D. oligosanthes* (few-flowered panicgrass). Thickets; FACU.

Dichanthelium xanthophysum

Dichanthelium oligosanthes

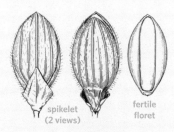

spikelet
(2 views)

fertile
floret

D. oligosanthes

fertile
floret
(2 views)

spikelet
(4 views)

D. xanthophysum

*In this treatment, *D. wrightianum* is included under *D. acuminatum*, while *D. lucidum* and *D. microcarpon* are includ-ed under *D. dichotomum*.

Note: Notes on keying *Dichanthelium* species (adapted from Weakley 2015):

For a node to be considered "bearded," it should have hairs that are longer and different in orientation and/ or structure than the hairs of the stems or sheaths. Lower nodes are the best place to look for this character. Nodes with short hairs are generally not considered bearded.

Use lower sheaths for identification purposes (but not the lowest sheath).

Do not use the lowest internode for identification purposes; it is typically uncharacteristic of the other internodes.

Do not consider the cilia on the margin of the sheath or leaves when deciding whether they are hairy or smooth.

For leaf characteristics, use the stem leaves.

For a leaf blade to be considered heart-shaped, the bottom part must extend outward and partially encircle the stem.

Examine at least three ligules before making a decision.

Use care in distinguishing ligule hair from the hairs at the base of the leaf and the marginal cilia. Ligule hairs arise from a cartilaginous base.

Measure spikelets from the bottom of the first glume to the tip of the second glume or sterile lemma (whichever is longer).

Digitaria (crabgrass)

A

If the inflorescence is a large, diffuse panicle, it is *D. cognata* [*Leptoloma cognatum*] (fall witchgrass). Sandy fields, roadsides.

If the inflorescence is ± digitate, like fingers on a hand, go to

 B

Digitaria cognata

fertile floret

spikelet (2 views)

D. cognata

B

If the fertile floret is brown-black to purplish, go to

 C

If the fertile floret is pale gray-brown or brown-tinged to white, go to

 D

C

If the rachis is sharply triangular, it is *D. filiformis* (slender crabgrass). Fields, roadsides, disturbed areas.

If the rachis is noticeably winged, it is *D. ischaemum*† (smooth crabgrass). Fields, lawns, disturbed areas; UPL.

Digitaria filiformis

Digitaria ischaemum

fertile floret | winged rachis | spikelet | **D. ischaemum**

fertile floret | spikelet | **D. filiformis**

D If the pedicels of the spikelets are sharply triangular and rough to the touch on the angles, go to **E**

If the pedicels of the spikelets are rounded and smooth, it is *D. serotina* (dwarf crabgrass). Sandy woodlands; FAC.

Digitaria serotina

fertile floret

pedicel
spikelet

D. serotina

E If the leaves are densely hairy, it is *D. sanguinalis*† (hairy crabgrass). Fields, roadsides, disturbed areas; FACU.

If the leaves are smooth (the upper leaf surface may be sparsely hairy near the base), it is *D. ciliaris* (southern crabgrass). Sandy fields, roadsides, disturbed areas; FACU/FAC.

Digitaria sanguinalis

Digitaria ciliaris

spikelet
(2 views)

D. sanguinalis

Echinochloa (barnyard grass)

A If the clusters of spikelets (racemes) are few and distant from one another (± 1 cm apart) along the rachis and the spikelets are awnless, it is *E. colona*† (awnless barnyard grass). Fields, ditches, disturbed wet areas; FACW.

If the clusters of spikelets are numerous, crowded, and overlapping, and the spikelets are awned or awnless, go to **B**

Echinochloa colona

cluster of spikelets

fertile floret
(2 views)

spikelet
(3 views)

E. colona

B If the second glume has an awn 2–10 mm long, the sterile lemma is usually long-awned, and the sheaths are usually papillate-hairy, it is *E. walteri* (coastal barnyard grass). Tidal marshes and mudflats of the coastal plain; OBL/FACW.

Echinochloa walteri

If the second glume is awnless or nearly so, the sterile lemma is awned or awnless, and the sheaths are smooth, go to **C**

E. walteri

C If the spikelets are covered with glandular spines arising from yellowish bumps (papillae) and the tip of the fertile lemma is firm, it is *E. muricata* (American barnyard grass). Moist ground, alluvial shores; FACW.

Echinochloa muricata

If the spikelets are smooth, hairy, or covered with slender spines (usually with no yellowish bumps at their base) and the fertile lemma has a withering tip that is offset by a line of hairs, go to **D**

spikelets (2 views showing papillae)

E. muricata

fertile floret with firm tip

D If the spikelets are grayish-purple, plump, and closely crowded, with awnless or awned-tipped sterile lemmas, it is *E. frumentacea*† (Siberian millet, billion dollar grass). Disturbed areas; UPL.

If the spikelets are greenish or purple-tinged, not so plump, and not so closely crowded, and the sterile lemmas are awnless (some may have ± well-developed awns), it is *E. crus-galli*† (barnyard grass). FACW/FAC.

Echinochloa frumentacea

Echinochloa crus-galli

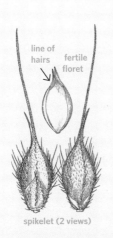

line of hairs   fertile floret

spikelet (2 views)

E. crus-galli

spikelet

E. frumentacea

113

Elymus (wildrye)

If there is mostly one spikelet per node, go to

If there are mostly two spikelets per node (side by side), go to

If the plant is rhizomatous, it is *E. repens*† [*Elytrigia repens*] (quackgrass). Roadsides, disturbed areas.

If the plant is tufted, it is *E. trachycaulus* (slender wheatgrass). Open woods, barrens, banks; FAC/FACU.

Elymus repens

Elymus trachycaulus

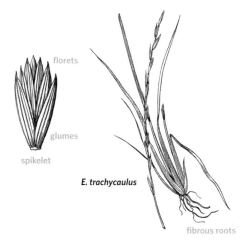

florets

glumes

spikelet

E. trachycaulus

fibrous roots

spikelet

E. repens   rhizome

If the glumes (if present) are bristlelike and 1–3 mm long, it is *E. hystrix* (bottlebrush grass). Forests, roadsides; UPL.

If the glumes are present and well developed (longer and broader), go to

Elymus hystrix

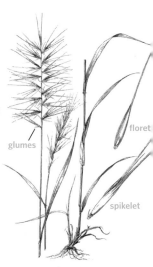

glumes

floret

spikelet

E. hystrix

D

If the glumes are leathery, flat, and striate (striped) at the base, it is *E. canadensis* (Great Plains wildrye). Moist forests; FAC/FACU.

Elymus canadensis

If the glumes are hard and rounded at the unstriped base, go to

E

spikelet

floret

E. canadensis

E

If the glumes are 1–2 mm wide and clearly flare out (get wider) above the base, it is *E. virginicus* (Virginia wildrye). Moist woods, meadows, prairies; FAC/FACW.

Elymus virginicus

Note: This is a polymorphic species with many varieties. Two closely related and recently described species, *E. macgregorii* and *E. glabriflorus*, are included in *E. virginicus* in this treatment.

If the glumes are < 1 mm wide and ± do not flare out above the base, go to

F

flared glumes

spikelet

E. virginicus

F

If the spikes are strongly nodding and there are 9-15 nodes per stem, it is *E. wiegandii* (northern riverbank wildrye). Rich alluvial soils in the shade.

Elymus wiegandii

If the spikes are erect to nodding and there are less than or equal to 10 nodes per stem, go to

G

spikelet

E. wiegandii

G If the the leaf blades have long, soft hairs on the upper surface (5-7 leaves/stem), it is *E. villosus* (downy wildrye). Stream banks, moist woods, marshes; FACU.

If the leaf blades are smooth to scabrous on the upper surface (8-10 leaves/stem), it is *E. riparius* (eastern riverbank wildrye). Moist forests, streambanks; FACW.

Elymus villosus

Elymus riparius

E. villosus

E. riparius

Eragrostis (lovegrass)

A If the plants form large mats, rooting at the nodes (decumbent), and . . .

the lemmas are small (1.5-2 mm long) and the pedicels are 1–3 mm long, it is *E. hypnoides* (teel lovegrass). Sandy shores, mudflats; OBL.

Eragrostis hypnoides

the lemmas are larger (2–4 mm long) and the pedicels are <1 mm long, it is *E. reptans* [*Neeragrostis reptans*] (creeping lovegrass). Rivers, lake margins; OBL.

If the plants do not form mats, go to **B**

Eragrostis reptans

persistent palea

seed   flore
spikelet with 2
florets (lower
floret without
lemma)

E. hypnoides

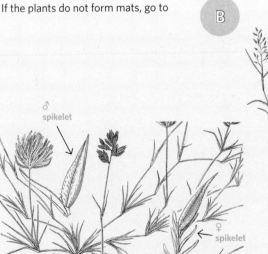

♂ spikelet

♀ spikelet

E. reptans

B

If there are scattered glandular dots along the leaf margins, go to **C**

If the leaf margins are not glandular, go to **D**

C

If the lemmas have glandular dots along the keel (check several lemmas), it is *E. cilianensis*† (stinkgrass). Various habitats; common weed; FACU.

If the lemmas do not have glandular dots along the keel, it is *E. minor*† (little lovegrass). Moist soils, wasteland, gardens, roadsides.

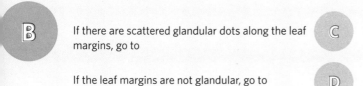

Eragrostis cilianensis

Eragrostis minor

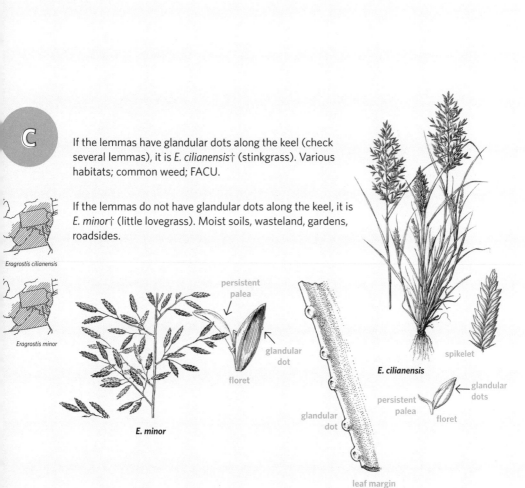

persistent palea

glandular dot

floret

E. minor

glandular dot

E. cilianensis

persistent palea

floret

glandular dots

spikelet

leaf margin

D

If the plant is a perennial, go to **E**

If the plant is an annual, go to **F**

If the spikelets are purple and . . .

there are seven to eleven florets per spikelet, it is *E. spectabilis* (purple lovegrass). Dry soils, fields, open woods; FACU/UPL.

Eragrostis spectabilis

there are eleven to twenty-eight florets per spikelet, it is *E. refracta* (coastal lovegrass). Moist or wet, sandy or muddy soils along the coast; FACW.

Eragrostis refracta

If the spikelets are not purple, go to

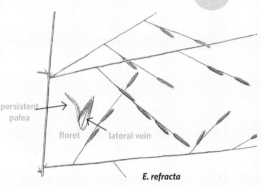

persistent palea

floret

lateral vein

E. refracta

spikelet

floret

E. spectabilis

If there are two to six florets per spikelet, go to

If there are usually more than six florets per spikelet (check several spikelets), go to

If the lateral veins of the lemma are inconspicuous, it is *E. hirsuta* (bigtop lovegrass). Dry sandy soils near the coast; FACU/UPL.

Eragrostis hirsuta

If the lateral veins of the lemma are conspicuous, go to

H

If the panicle is large and diffuse, making up two-thirds or more of the plant's height, it is *E. capillaris* (lacegrass). Open woods, dry soils.

If the panicle is open but smaller, making up about half of the plant's height, it is *E. frankii* (sandbar lovegrass). Riverbanks, sandbars, moist ground; FACW.

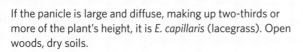

persistent palea   floret

Eragrostis capillaris

E. capillaris

Eragrostis frankii

spikelet

E. frankii

spikelet

I

If the spikelets are appressed to the panicle branches, it is *E. pectinacea* (tufted lovegrass). Moist ground, a weed in gardens and waste places; FAC.

If the spikelets diverge from the panicle branches and . . .

the leaves are narrow (1–3 mm wide), it is *E. pilosa*† (India lovegrass). Fields, roadsides, disturbed areas; common; FACU.

the leaves are broader (3–6 mm wide), it is *E. mexicana* (Mexican lovegrass). Open woods, dry soils.

E. pectinacea

Eragrostis pectinacea

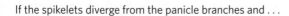
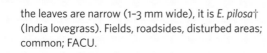
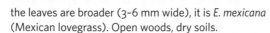

Eragrostis pilosa

Eragrostis mexicana

persistent palea

floret

E. pilosa

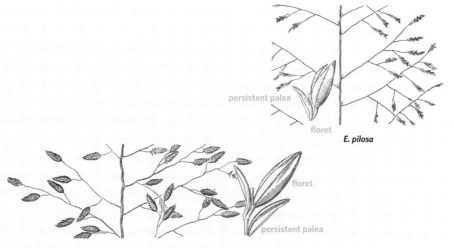

floret

persistent palea

E. mexicana

If there are five to nine florets per pair of glumes, it is *E. curvula*† (weeping lovegrass). Cultivated and escaped. .

If there are eleven to twenty-eight florets per pair of glumes, it is *E. refracta* (coastal lovegrass). Moist or wet, sandy or muddy soils along the coast; FACW. See page 118.

Eragrostis curvula

lateral vein

floret

E. curvula

Festuca/Schedonorus (fescue)

If the leaves have large, prominent, clawlike or curved and sometimes undulating auricles and . . .

the auricles have a fringe of hairs and the internodes of the rachilla are scabrous, it is *Schedonorus arundinaceus*† [*Festuca elatior*] (tall fescue). Roadsides, fields, open ground.

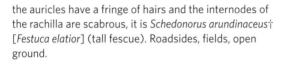

Schedonorus arundinaceus

the auricles are smooth and the internodes of the rachilla are smooth, it is *Schedonorus pratensis*† [*Festuca pratensis*] (meadow fescue). Fields, meadows, moist soils; FACU.

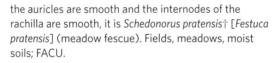

Schedonorus pratensis

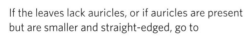

If the leaves lack auricles, or if auricles are present but are smaller and straight-edged, go to **B**

floret

spikelet

Schedonorus arundinaceus

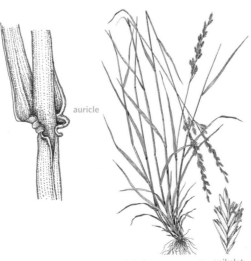

auricle

Schedonorus pratensis spikelet

B If the leaf blades are flat, ≥ 3 mm wide, and . . .

the spikelets are clustered at the ends of the panicle branches and overlap one another, it is *F. paradoxa* (cluster fescue). Moist or wet open woods and prairies; FAC.

Festuca paradoxa

the spikelets are scattered along the panicle branches (barely touching the bottom of the spikelet above), it is *F. subverticillata* [*F. obtusa*] (nodding fescue). Moist woods; FACU.

Festuca subverticillata

If the leaf blades are curled or folded and are < 3 mm wide, go to **C**

floret

F. paradoxa

glumes

3 florets

F. subverticillata

C If the leaf blades are wiry and the lemmas are awnless or with a short awn (< 0.5 mm), it is *F. filiformis*† [*F. tenuifolia*] (hair fescue). Lawns, waste places.

Festuca filiformis

If the leaf blades are narrow but not wiry and the awn of the lemma is usually ≥ 1 mm, go to **D**

floret

F. filiformis

D If the basal sheaths are closed, purple to reddish-brown and disintegrate into shredded fibers as they age, it is *F. rubra* (red fescue). Wide range of open habitats; FACU.

Festuca rubra

If the basal sheaths are open and overlapping, pale or brown and remain intact as they age, go to E

floret

spikelet

F. rubra

E If the spikelets are mostly ≤ 7 mm long, it is *F. ovina*† (sheep fescue). Open woods, dry fields, roadsides; UPL.

If the spikelets are mostly ≥ 7 mm long, it is *F. trachyphylla*† [*F. brevipila*] (hard fescue). Dry, open soils; UPL.

Festuca ovina

Festuca trachyphylla

floret

F. ovina

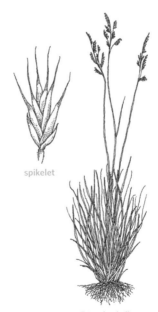

spikelet

F. trachyphylla

Glyceria (mannagrass)

If the spikelets are long, narrow, and cylindrical, go to

If the spikelets are rounded, go to

If the lemma is pointed and much shorter than the forked palea, it is *G. acutiflora* (creeping mannagrass). Shallow water, mucky soils, wet pastures; OBL.

If the lemma is rounded, equal to or only slightly shorter than the palea in length, and . . .

Glyceria acutiflora

the spikelets are very rough when brushed backward with a finger and the lemmas are dull and scabrous between the veins, it is *G. septentrionalis* (northern mannagrass). Shallow water, wet mucky soils, cypress ponds; OBL.

Glyceria septentrionalis

the spikelets are smooth to slightly rough when brushed backward with a finger and the lemmas are smooth, green, and shining between the scabrous veins, it is *G. borealis* (northern mannagrass). Shallow water, wet soils; OBL.

Glyceria borealis

floret   spikelet

G. acutiflora

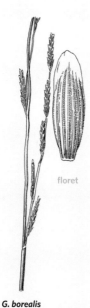

floret

G. borealis

floret

G. septentrionalis

C

If the panicle branches are ascending and ± appressed to the rachis, and . . .

the panicle is dense, compact, cylindrical (≤ 15 cm long) and upright, it is *G. obtusa* (Atlantic mannagrass). Swamp forests, wet meadows, freshwater marshes mainly near the coast; OBL.

Glyceria obtusa

the panicle is slender and elongate (5–36 cm long) and nodding to drooping, it is *G. melicaria* (melic mannagrass). Swamp forests; OBL.

If the panicle is open with drooping branches, go to **D**

Glyceria melicaria

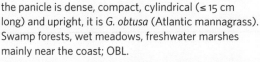

floret (2 views)

G. melicaria

floret (2 views)

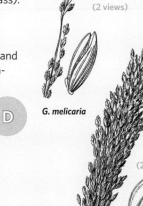

G. obtusa

D

If the lemma is conspicuously longer than the palea (by at least 0.5 mm), and the florets are ± round, it is *G. canadensis* (rattlesnake mannagrass). Bogs, wet meadows; OBL.

If the lemma is ± equal to or only slightly longer than the palea and the florets are elliptical, go to **E**

Glyceria canadensis

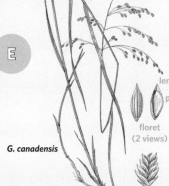

lemma

palea

floret (2 views)

G. canadensis

spikelet

E

If the spikelets are ≥4 mm long, the first glume is > 1 mm long, and the second glume is ≥ 1.5 mm long, it is *G. grandis* (American mannagrass). Wet, mucky soils of open wetlands; OBL.

If the spikelets are smaller (≤ 4 mm long), the first glume is ≤ 1 mm long, and the second glume is ≤ 1.3 mm long, it is *G. striata* (ridged mannagrass). Wet meadows, bogs, marshes, swamp forests; OBL.

Glyceria grandis

Glyceria striata

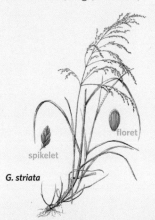

floret

spikelet

G. striata

spikelet

G. grandis

Gymnopogon (skeletongrass)

Gymnopogon
ambiguus

Gymnopogon
brevifolius

G. ambiguus (bearded skeletongrass) lemma smooth to sparsely hairy on midvein. Awn of lemma > 4 mm long. Serpentine barrens, dry fields, dry pinelands and woodlands.

G. brevifolius (shortleaf skeletongrass) lemma densely hairy on midvein and margins. Awn of lemma < 2 mm long. Dry woodlands, prairies, sandhills, pine savannahs, calcareous glades; FACU.

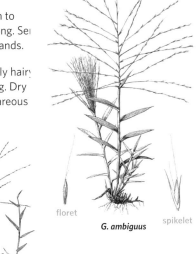

floret

spikelet

G. ambiguus

floret

glumes

spikelet

G. brevifolius

Holcus (velvetgrass)

Holcus lanatus

Holcus mollis

H. lanatus† (velvetgrass). Portion of stem below node hairy. Pastures, disturbed areas, roadsides; common; FACU/FAC regionwide).

H. mollis† (creeping velvetgrass). Stems smooth except for bearded nodes. Lawns; FACU.

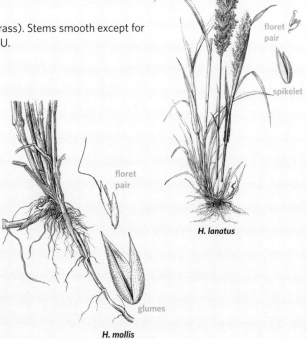

floret
pair

spikelet

floret
pair

glumes

H. lanatus

H. mollis

Hordeum [*Critesion*] (barley)

If the glumes of the central spikelet are bristlelike and plant is perennial, it is *H. jubatum* [*C. jubatum*] (foxtail barley). Dry, old fields, roadsides, disturbed areas; FAC.

Hordeum jubatum

If the glumes of the central spikelet are broader (> 0.5 mm wide and plants are annual), go to B

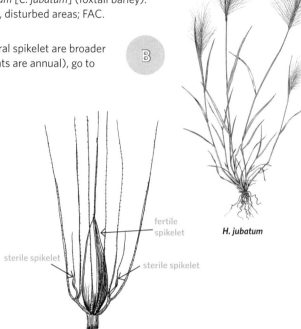

fertile spikelet

sterile spikelet

sterile spikelet

3 spikelets side by side

H. jubatum

 B

If the glumes of the central spikelet are short-haired on the margins, it is *H. murinum*† [*C. murinum*] (wall barley). Disturbed areas; UPL.

If the glumes of the central spikelet are smooth to scabrous-margined, it is *H. pusillum* [*C. pusillum*] (little barley). Roadside banks, ditches, disturbed areas; FACU/FAC.

Tip: In noncultivated barley, the lateral spikelets are pedicellate, sterile, and narrower than the center spikelet; the center spikelet is fertile and plump.

Hordeum murinum

Hordeum pusillum

glumes of fertile spikelet (hairy)

spikelet triad

H. murinum

H. pusillum

Leersia (cutgrass)

A

If there are two to three lower panicle branches per node and the leaves and sheaths are scabrous, it is *L. oryzoides* (rice cutgrass). Marshes, riverbanks, pond shores; OBL.

Leersia oryzoides

If there is one lower panicle branch per node and the leaves and sheaths are smooth to scabrous, go to **B**

overlapping spikelets

floret

L. oryzoides

B

If the spikelets are round, it is *L. lenticularis* (catchfly grass). Floodplain forests, swamps; OBL.

If the spikelets are elliptical to elongate, go to **C**

Leersia lenticularis

over-lapping spikelets

L. lenticularis

C

If the panicle is strict with erect, ascending branches, it is *L. hexandra* (southern cutgrass). Plants of open wet habitats such as ponds, lakes, pools in the coastal plain; OBL.

If the panicle is open with spreading branches, it is *L. virginica* (white cutgrass). Plants of shaded wet habitats such as floodplain forests, swamps, streambanks; FACW.

Leersia hexandra

Leersia virginica

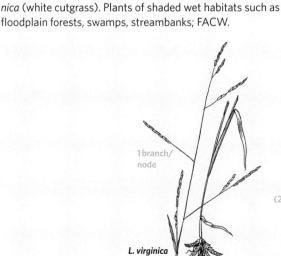

1 branch/ node

floret (2 views)

L. virginica

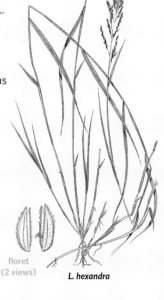

L. hexandra

Leptochloa (sprangletop)

Leptochloa fusca

Leptochloa panicea

L. fusca (bearded sprangletop). Sheaths smooth to scabrous. (Ours is ssp. *fascicularis*, introduced from southern North America.) Railroad sidings, waste ground; FACW.

L. panicea (sprangletop). Sheaths sparsely to densely hairy, hairs papillose-based. Disturbed areas; FACW.

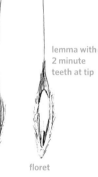

L. fusca

floret

spikelet

lemma with 2 minute teeth at tip

floret

L. panicea

Lolium (ryegrass)

A If the spikelets have ≤ ten florets, go to **B**

If the spikelets have eleven to twenty-two florets, it is *L. multiflorum*† (annual ryegrass). Fields, roadsides, pastures, disturbed areas.

Lolium multiflorum

floret

spikelet

L. multiflorum

B

If the plant is an annual, the spikelets have two to ten florets, and the glume is ± as long as or exceeding the the spikelet, it is *L. temulentum*† (darnel). Fields, roadsides, pastures, disturbed areas; common.

If the plant is a perennial, the spikelets have five to nine florets, and the glume is markedly shorter than the spikelet, it is *L. perenne*† (perennial ryegrass). Fields, roadsides, pastures, disturbed areas; common; FACU.

Lolium temulentum

Lolium perenne

spikelet   **L. temulentum**

L. perenne

Melica (melic)

M. mutica (two-flower melic). Glumes are ± equal and oblong. Forests, woodlands.

M. nitens (three-flower melic). Glumes are markedly unequal; first glume is very broad, and its margins meet around the spikelet. Rocky upland woodlands, barrens, glades.

Melica mutica

Melica nitens

spikelet

M. mutica   rudimentary lemma (uppermost 1–4 lemmas are rudimentary and smaller than the fertile ones)

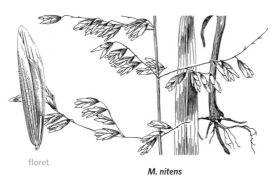

floret

M. nitens

Muhlenbergia (muhly)

A If both glumes are shorter than the lemma, go to **B**

If at least 1 glume is about as long or longer than the lemma, go to **C**

Muhlenbergia schreberi

If the first glume is ± absent and the second glume is a minute stub, it is *M. schreberi* (nimblewill). Woods, thickets, waste ground; FAC.

glumes (use magnification)

floret   spikelet

M. schreberi

B If the plant is rhizomatous, go to **D**

If the plant is tufted, go to **E**

C If the glumes are much longer than the lemma, it is *M. glomerata* (spike muhly). Wet rocky hillsides and seeps, marshes, fens, calcareous wet ground; FACW.

Muhlenbergia glomerata

If the glumes are about as long as the lemma (*M. frondosa* may be slightly longer), go to **F**

floret

bearded callus

glumes

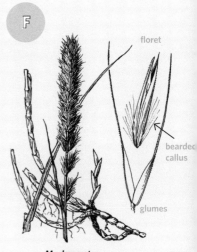

M. glomerata

D   If the glumes are only slightly shorter than the floret, go to

If the glumes are much shorter than the floret, go to

E   If the inflorescence is open and the branches and/or spikelets are purple, go to

Muhlenbergia cuspidata

If the inflorescence is slender and spikelike, and the spikelets are sometimes purple, it is *M. cuspidata* (plains muhly). Alluvial shores, rock crevices.

floret

glumes

M. cuspidata

F   If the panicle is open and diffuse, go to

If the panicle is slender, contracted, and often dense (the plant itself can have numerous branches, but the panicles are not diffuse/open), go to

G

If the inflorescence is slender and the spikelets are sessile or nearly so, it is *M. mexicana* (wirestem muhly). Woods, rocky shores, swamps, serpentine barrens; FAC/FACW.

If the inflorescence is looser and the spikelets are borne on pedicels up to and equaling their length, it is *M. sylvatica* (woodland muhly). Moist woods, shaded banks; FACW/FAC.

Muhlenbergia mexicana

Muhlenbergia sylvatica

spikelet

M. mexicana

floret   glumes

M. sylvatica

H

If the internodes (the part of the stem between the nodes) and sheaths are smooth, it is *M. sobolifera* (rock muhly). Dry, rocky slopes; serpentine barrens.

If the internodes and usually the base of the sheaths are hairy, it is *M. tenuiflora* (slimflowered muhly). Rocky, wooded slopes, along streams; FACU.

Muhlenbergia sobolifera

Muhlenbergia tenuiflora

M. sobolifera

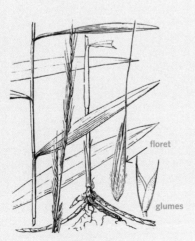

floret

glumes

glumes   floret

M. tenuiflora

Muhlenbergia
capillaris

Muhlenbergia uniflora

I

If the spikelets are > 2 mm long (not including the awns), it is *M. capillaris* (hairy-awned muhly). River shores; FAC/FACU.

If the spikelets are smaller (≤ 2 mm long), it is *M. uniflora* (bog muhly). Marshes, bogs, moist, sandy roadsides; OBL.

M. capillaris

M. uniflora

J

If the ligule is a ring of hairs (sheaths strongly flattened), it is *M. torreyana* (New Jersey muhly). Moist pine barrens; coastal.

If the ligule is membranous and irregularly toothed (spikelets often purplish or blackish), it is *M. asperifolia* (scratchgrass). Waste ground; inland; FACW (native to western and midwestern United States).

Muhlenbergia
torreyana

Muhlenbergia
asperifolia

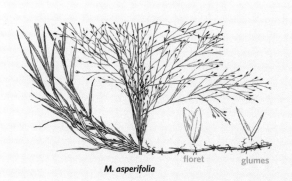

M. asperifolia

M. torreyana

K

If the plant has prominent, scaly rhizomes, go to L

If the plant lacks prominent, scaly rhizomes, it is *M. cuspidata.* See page 131.

 L

If the plant has numerous branches with numerous axillary (often partly hidden) panicles, it is *M. frondosa* (wirestem muhly). Moist, open woods and streambanks; common; FAC.

Muhlenbergia frondosa

If the plant has few elongated branches with visible panicles, go to M

floret

glumes

M. frondosa

 M

If the spikelets are borne on pedicels up to or equaling their length, it is *M. sylvatica.* See page 132.

If the spikelets are sessile or nearly so, it is *M. mexicana.* See page 132.

Panicum (panicgrass)

A   If the spikelet is covered with warty bumps, it is *P. verrucos-um* (warty panicgrass). Wet woods and shores mostly on the coastal plain; FACW.

If the spikelet is not covered in warty bumps, go to **B**

Panicum verrucosum

fertile
floret

spikelet
(2 views)

P. verrucosum

B   If the panicle is < 2 cm wide at maturity, go to **C**

If the panicle is > 2 cm wide at maturity, go to **D**

C   If the spikelets are > 4 mm long and the ligule is > 1 mm long, it is *P. amarum* (bitter beachgrass). Coastal dunes, shores; FAC/FACU (grasses with bluish-green leaves).

If the spikelets are < 4 mm long and the ligule is < 1 mm long, go to **E**

Panicum amarum

spikelet

P. amarum

D If the plant is a perennial (rhizomatous or with a hard, knotty crown), go to

If the plant is an annual (look for a cluster of fibrous roots), go to

E If the tip of the fertile palea is not enclosed by the fertile lemma, it is *P. hemitomon* (maidencane). Swamps and ponds on the coastal plain; OBL/FACW.

If the tip of the fertile palea is enclosed by the fertile lemma, it is *P. anceps* (beaked panicgrass). Moist, sandy soils; FAC.

Panicum hemitomon

Panicum anceps

fertile floret

spikelet

P. anceps

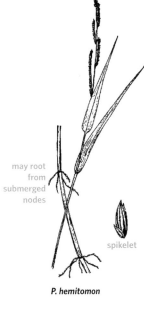

may root from submerged nodes

spikelet

P. hemitomon

F If the plant is rhizomatous and the stems are slightly flattened to round (test by rolling between the fingers), go to

Panicum rigidulum

If the plant has a hard knotty crown (no rhizomes) and the stems are strongly flattened, it is *P. rigidulum* (redtop panicum). Wet soils; FACW.

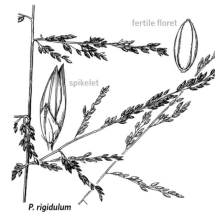

fertile floret

spikelet

P. rigidulum

If the sheaths are hairy, go to

If the sheaths are smooth, it is *P. dichotomiflorum* (fall panicum). Moist soils and shores, weedy; FACW.

Panicum dichotomiflorum

fertile floret

spikelet

spikelet

P. dichotomiflorum

If the stems are slightly flattened to round and the spikelets are ± secund (on one side of the rachis) and < 4 mm long, it is *P. anceps* (beaked panicgrass). See page 136.

If the stems are round and the spikelets are not secund and are usually > 4 mm long, go to

If the spikelets are ≥ 4.5 mm long and plump, it is *P. miliaceum* (broomcorn). Cultivated and adventive to roadsides and disturbed areas.

If the spikelets are < 4 mm long, go to

Panicum miliaceum

fertile floret

spikelet (2 views)

P. miliaceum

Panicum virgatum

J

If the panicle is narrow with erect branches, it is *P. amarum*. See page 135.

If the panicle is large and diffuse, it is *P. virgatum* (switchgrass). Open woods, prairies, dunes, shores, brackish marshes; FAC.

fertile flor

spikelet
(2 views)

P. virgatum

Panicum flexile

K

If the panicle is diffuse (less than twice as long as it is wide), go to

 L

If the panicle is narrower (two to three times as long as it is wide), it is *P. flexile* (wiry witch grass). Moist or dry soils, often in open woods; FAC/FACU.

fertile floret

spikelet (2 views)

P. flexile

L

If the fertile lemmas are blackish, it is *P. philadelphicum* (panic grass). Dry soils and sandy fields; FAC.

If the fertile lemmas are yellowish, it is *P. capillare* (witch grass). Weed in fields and gardens; FAC.

*Panicum
philadelphicum*

Panicum capillare

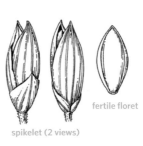

fertile floret

spikelet (2 views)

P. philadelphicum

fertile
floret (2
views)

spikelet
(3 views)

P. capillare

Paspalum (paspalum)

Tip: In *Paspalum*, the first glume is absent or, if present, very short.

If the rachis is broad and is folded over the spikelets, and . . .

Panicum dissectum

the inflorescence comprises few (2-5) racemes, it is *P. dissectum* (mudbank paspalum). Shallow water and muddy shores on the coastal plain; OBL.

the inflorescence comprises many (20-50) racemes, it is *P. repens* [*P. fluitans*] (water paspalum). Lakes, streams, roadside ditches; OBL.

Panicum repens

If the rachis is narrow and not folded over the spikelets, go to **B**

spikelet (2 views)

P. dissectum   fertile floret

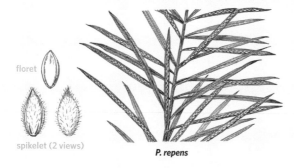
floret

spikelet (2 views)

P. repens

If the inflorescence is a pair of racemes that are < 1 cm apart at their point of attachment to the rachis, it is *P. distichum* [*P. paspalodes*] (knotgrass). Swamps, wet ground, waste places; OBL/FACW.

Panicum distichum

If there is a single, terminal raceme or two or more racemes spaced > 1 cm apart at their point of attachment to the rachis, go to **C**

P. distichum

C   If the spikelets are hairy, go to **D**

If the spikelets are smooth, go to **E**

D   If the spikelets are long-haired, especially at the margin, it is *P. dilatatum*† (dallisgrass). Roadsides, fields, disturbed areas; FAC.

If the spikelets are short-haired add (often brown mottled), it is *P. setaceum* (thin paspalum). Dry or moist, open or lightly wooded places; FAC/FACU.

Panicum dilatatum

Panicum setaceum

fertile floret

spikelet (2 views)

P. setaceum

spikelet

P. dilatatum

E   If the stems are flattened, it is *P. pubiflorum* (hairyseed paspalum). Moist or wet soils; FACW/FAC.

If the stems are round, go to **F**

Panicum pubiflorum

fertile floret

spikelet (2 views)

P. pubiflorum

F

If the fertile lemma is dark brown, it is *P. boscianum* (bull paspalum). Moist or wet soils; FACW.

If the fertile lemma is yellow to pale brown, go to **G**

Panicum boscianum

fertile floret

spikelet (2 views)

P. boscianum

G

If the plants are tall and stout, and usually 1–2 m in height, it is *P. floridanum* (Florida paspalum). Moist, sandy soils on the coastal plain; FACW.

If the plants are low-growing and < 1 m in height, go to **H**

Panicum floridanum

fertile floret

spikelet (2 views)

P. floridanum

H

If the sterile lemma is five-veined, it is *P. laeve* (field paspalum). Various habitats; FACW/FAC.

If the sterile lemma is two- to three-veined, it is *P. setaceum* (thin paspalum). Dry or moist, open or lightly wooded places; FAC/FACU. See page 140.

Panicum laeve

fertile floret

spikelet (2 views)

P. laeve

Phalaris (canarygrass)

Phalaris arundinacea

Phalaris canariensis

P. arundinacea (reed canarygrass). Inflorescence is branched or lobed, often suffused with purple, and the glumes are not winged. Moist forests, moist disturbed areas, marshes; common; OBL/FACW.

P. canariensis† (annual canarygrass). Ornamental; inflorescence is dense, ellipsoid, and not lobed or branched, and the glumes are winged. Disturbed areas; FACU.

fertile
floret

sterile
lemmas

glumes

P. canariensis

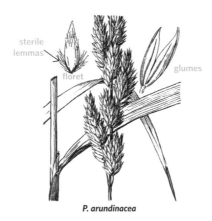

sterile
lemmas

floret

glumes

P. arundinacea

Piptatherum (piptatherum, ricegrass)

A

If the lemma is shiny and dark brown to black when mature, it is *P. racemosum* [*Oryzopsis racemosa, Patis racemosa*] (mountain ricegrass). Calcareous woodlands and forests; common.

*Piptatherum
racemosum*

If the lemma is tan to yellowish when mature, go to

B

floret   *P. racemosum*

B

If the awn of the lemma is short (1–2 mm or frequently absent), it is *P. pungens* [*Oryzopsis pungens*] (sharp pip-tatherum). Dry, rocky, or sandy woods.

If the awn is long (6–11 mm), it is *P. canadense* [*Oryzopsis canadensis*] (Canadian piptatherum). Sandy barrens.

Piptatherum pungens

Piptatherum canadense

P. pungens

floret

floret

glumes

P. canadense

Poa (bluegrass)

A

If all or most of the lemmas are modified into plump, pur-plish bulblets, it is *P. bulbosa*† (bulbous bluegrass). Waste ground; FACU.

If the lemmas are not modified into bulblets, go to **B**

Poa bulbosa

bulblet

P. bulbosa

B If the lemma has cobwebby hairs at the base (pull out an individual lemma and examine with a ten-power hand lens), go to **C**

If there are no cobwebby hairs at the base of the lemma—don't confuse these with hairs on the veins—and . . .

Poa annua

the plant is an annual with lemmas hairy only on the veins, it is *P. annua†* (annual bluegrass). Fields, roadsides, lawns, disturbed areas; common; FACU.

Poa autumnalis

the plant is a perennial with lemmas hairy on the veins and between the veins, at least on the lower part of the floret, it is *P. autumnalis* (autumn bluegrass). Moist to dry forests; FAC.

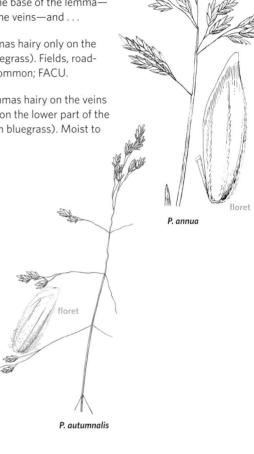

floret

P. annua

floret

P. autumnalis

C If the plant is an annual, it is *P. chapmaniana* (Chapman's bluegrass). Fields, roadsides, disturbed areas; FACU/UPL.

If the plant is a perennial (tufted or rhizomatous), go to **D**

Poa chapmaniana

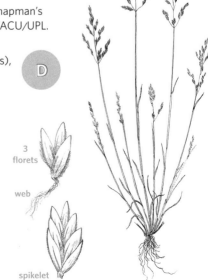

3 florets

web

spikelet

P. chapmaniana

If the stems are flattened and keeled, it is *P. compressa*†
(Canada bluegrass). Dry woods, fields, rock outcrops;
FACU.

If the stems are round (test by rolling between the
fingers), go to

Poa compressa

Tip: The hairs on the lemmas of *Poa* may be hard to
observe with just a hand
lens. If necessary, collect
the specimen (including the
belowground parts) and use
a dissecting scope.

stem cross section

floret   **P. compressa**

If the lemmas are smooth, it is *P. saltuensis* (oldpasture
bluegrass). Forests, woodlands, barrens, glades.

If the lemmas are hairy or scabrous only on the
keel (at least on the lower part), go to

If the lemmas are hairy on the keel and/or on the
marginal veins (at least at the bottom portion),
go to

Poa saltuensis

Poa sylvestris

If the entire lemma is hairy, it is *P. sylvestris* (woodland
bluegrass). Rich woods; FACW.

Note: Don't confuse this with *P. cuspidata*, which is ± hairy
on the veins but not between the veins.

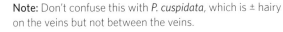

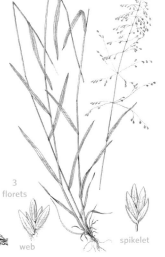

3
florets

web   spikelet

P. sylvestris

floret

web

P. saltuensis

F

If the intermediate veins of the lemma are sharply conspicuous, it is *P. trivialis*† (rough bluegrass). Cultivated and frequently established in wet meadows, swamps, alluvial woods; FACW.

If the intermediate veins of the lemma are inconspicuous, it is *P. alsodes* (grove bluegrass). Cool, moist woods, thickets; UPL/FACW.

Poa trivialis

Poa alsodes

3 florets

web

glumes

P. trivialis

floret

web

spikelet

P. alsodes

G

If the panicle branches are mostly in pairs, go to   **H**

If the panicle branches are in whorls of three or more, go to   **I**

H

If the plant is growing in a wetland, it is *P. paludigena* (eastern bog bluegrass). Boggy woods, swamps; FACW.

If the plant is growing in an upland, it is *P. cuspidata* (early bluegrass). Dry, wooded hillsides, banks.

Poa paludigena

Poa cuspidata

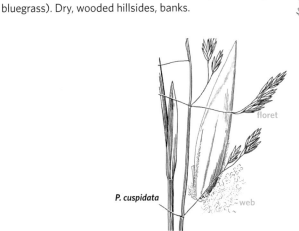

floret

P. cuspidata

web

floret

P. paludigena

web

146

If the plant has creeping rhizomes, it is *P. pratensis*† (Kentucky bluegrass). Cultivated and naturalized in meadows, roadsides, open woods, waste ground; FACU.

If the plant is tufted (may be loosely tufted), go to **J**

Poa pratensis

floret

web

spikelet

P. pratensis

If the ligule is 0.5 mm long, it is *P. nemoralis*† (woodland bluegrass). Dry woods and edges; scattered; FAC.

If the ligule ≥ 1mm long, go to **K**

Poa nemoralis

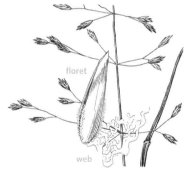

floret

web

P. nemoralis

If the ligule is 1 mm long and the intermediate veins are distinct, it is *P. sylvestris* (woodland bluegrass). See page 145.

If the ligule is 2.5–5 mm long and the intermediate veins are obscure, it is *P. palustris* (fowl bluegrass). Wet meadows, shores, thickets; FAC/FACW.

Poa palustris

floret

web

P. palustris

Puccinellia (alkali grass)

Puccinellia distans

Puccinellia fasciculata

P. distans† (European alkali grass). Inflorescence is ± open, and the midvein of the lemma does not reach the tip. Disturbed, salted roadsides and coastal sands; OBL.

P. fasciculata (Borrer's saltmarsh grass). Inflorescence is narrow, and the midvein of the lemma reaches the tip. Salt or brackish marshes; OBL.

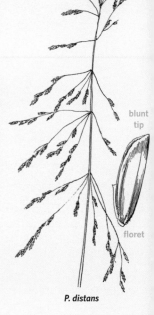

blunt tip

blunt tip

floret

floret

P. fasciculata

P. distans

Saccharum (plumegrass)

A

If the stem immediately below the inflorescence is covered with long, soft, appressed hairs, go to **B**

If the stem immediately below the inflorescence is smooth, go to **C**

B

If the awn is coiled at the base and the callus hairs are silvery to yellowish-brown, it is *S. alopecuroides* (silver plumegrass). Moist soils, fencerows, old fields; FAC.

If the awn is ± straight, not coiled, and the callus hairs are yellowish-brown to purple, it is *S. giganteum* (sugarcane plumegrass). Moist ground, old fields; FACW.

Saccharum alopecuroides

Saccharum giganteum

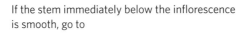

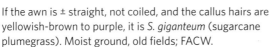

S. giganteum

spikelet

spikelet

S. alopecuroides

If the panicle is narrow with appressed branches and the callus hairs are absent (or, if present, few and short), it is *S. baldwinii* (narrow plumegrass). Shaded rivers and stream bottoms; OBL.

Saccharum baldwinii

If the panicle is looser with ascending to spreading branches and the callus hairs are dense, go to

If the awns are round at the base (straight to wavy) and the spikelets are dark brown, it is *S. coarctatum* (compressed plumegrass). Marshes, ditches, swamps.

Saccharum coarctatum

If the awns are flattened at the base (sometimes spirally coiled) and the spikelets are yellow to purplish, it is *S. brevibarbe* (shortbeard plumegrass). Open woodlands and forests, woodland borders; FACW/OBL.

Saccharum brevibarbe

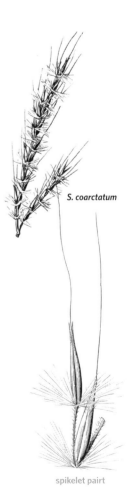

S. coarctatum

spikelet pairt

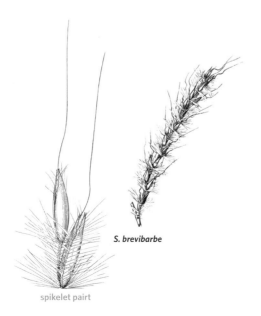

S. brevibarbe

spikelet pairt

149

Setaria (foxtail grass, bristlegrass)

If the inflorescence is erect and there are mostly four to twelve bristles beneath each spikelet, go to

If the inflorescence is erect, curved or nodding, and there are one to three bristles beneath each spikelet (*S. faberi* with nodding inflorescences can have up to six), go to

If the stems arise from a tuft and the root system is fibrous, it is *S. pumila*† [*S. glauca*] (yellow foxtail). Fields, gardens, roadsides; FAC.

If the stems arise separately along a knotty rhizome, it is *S. parviflora* [*S. geniculata*] (perennial foxtail, knotroot bristlegrass). Dry to moist, open soils; FACW/FAC.

Setaria pumila

Setaria parviflora

spikelet   floret

S. parviflora

S. pumila

If the fertile lemma is strongly to very finely horizontally wrinkled, go to

If the fertile lemma is smooth (may have longitudinal lines), go to

If the bristles of the inflorescence are rough to the touch when brushed upward, it is *S. verticillata*† (bristly foxtail, hooked bristlegrass). Waste ground, roadsides; FAC.

Setaria verticillata

If the bristles of inflorescence are rough to the touch when brushed downward, go to

sterile bristle

spikelet

S. verticillata

If the seed falls without the glumes and sterile lemma, go to

Setaria viridis

If the seed falls with the accompanying glumes and sterile lemma, it is *S. viridis*† (green foxtail, green bristlegrass). Cultivated fields, gardens, waste ground.

sterile bristle

fertile floret

spikelet

S. viridis

If the leaf blades are hairy and scabrous on the upper surface, it is *S. faberi*† (Chinese foxtail). Cultivated fields, roadsides, waste ground; UPL.

Setaria faberi

If the the leaf blades are only scabrous on the upper surface, it is *S. viridis*. See above.

S. faberi

G

If the fertile lemma is yellow to pale green, it is *S. italica*† (foxtail millet). Must examine a mature specimen. Cultivated; widespread; FACU.

If the fertile lemma is light brown, it is *S. magna* (giant bristlegrass). Salt marshes, interdune swales, coastal marshes; FACW.

Setaria italica

Setaria magna

S. italica

sterile
bristle

spikelet

fertile floret
(2 views)

S. magna

Sorghum (sorghum, Johnsongrass)

Sorghum bicolor

Sorghum halepense

S. bicolor† (shattercane). Annual, with leaves > 2 cm wide. Cultivated and escaped; FACU/UPL.

S. halepense† (Johnsongrass). Rhizomatous perennial, with leaves ≤ 2 cm wide. Noxious weed. Cultivated fields, roadsides, waste places; FACU.

spikelet pair

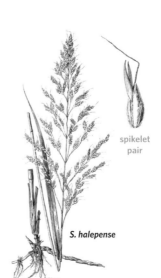

spikelet
pair

S. halepense

S. bicolor

Spartina (cordgrass)

A If the main leaf blades are curled under and are < 5 mm wide (flatten out to measure, or flatten and measure one side and double the measurement), it is *S. patens* (salt-meadow cordgrass). Upper edges of marshes and dunes in the coastal plain; FACW.

If the main leaf blades are flat or curled under when dry and are > 5 mm wide, go to **B**

Spartina patens

S. patens

B If the inflorescence branches are appressed to the rachis, making the inflorescence appear spikelike, it is *S. alterniflora* (smooth cordgrass). Salt marshes, coastal plain; OBL.

If the inflorescence branches are ascending to spreading, go to **C**

Spartina alterniflora

spikelet

S. alterniflora

C If the second glume is pointed but not awned (grasses from 1–3 m in height), it is *S. cynosuroides* (big cordgrass). Brackish and freshwater tidal marshes in the coastal plain; OBL.

If the second glume is awned (grasses from 1–2 m in height), it is *S. pectinata* (prairie cordgrass). Along waterways, grasslands, tidal freshwater marshes; OBL.

S. cynosuroides

Spartina pectinata

floret   spikelet

S. cynosuroides

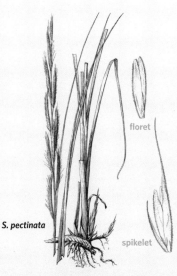

S. pectinata

floret

spikelet

Sphenopholis (wedgegrass)

Tip: The spikelets of *Sphenopholis* are strongly compressed.

If the spikelets are ≥ to 5 mm long and the upper lemma has a long awn (> 3.5 mm), it is *S. pensylvanica* (swamp oats). Swamps, wet woods; OBL.

Sphenopholis pensylvanica

If the spikelets are ≤ 5 mm and the upper lemma is awnless or short awned (< 3.5 mm long), go to **B**

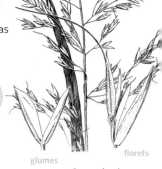

glumes

florets

S. pensylvanica

If the lower leaf blades are usually < 2mm wide and rolled under at the margins, it is *S. filiformis* (southern wedge-grass). Pine savannas, sandy woodlands, coastal plain; FACU/UPL.

Sphenopholis filiformis

If the lower leaf blades are flat and ≥ 2 mm wide, go to **C**

florets

glumes

S. filiformis

If the second lemma is very scabrous and the first glume is one-third to two-thirds as wide as the second glume, it is *S. nitida* (shiny wedgegrass). Dry to moist woods, hillsides, bottomlands; UPL/FAC.

Sphenopholis nitida

If the second lemma is smooth to slightly scabrous and the first glume is < one-third as wide as the second glume, go to **D**

florets

glumes

S. nitida

floret

glumes

D

If the panicle is loosely open and usually nodding, it is *S. intermedia* (slender wedgegrass). Moist forests; FAC.

If the panicle is compact and spikelike, it is *S. obtusata* (prairie wedgegrass). Moist meadows, streambanks, shores of ponds or lakes; FAC.

Sphenopholis intermedia

Sphenopholis obtusata

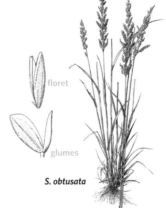

floret

glumes

S. intermedia

S. obtusata

Sporobolus (dropseed)

A

If the panicle is open, with branches spreading to appressed, go to **B**

If the panicle is slender and spikelike, go to **C**

B

If the leaf sheaths have a conspicuous tuft of long, white hairs at the top, it is *S. cryptandrus* (sand dropseed). Sandy soils in a variety of habitats; UPL.

Sporobolus cryptandrus

If the top of the leaf sheath is smooth or if a tuft of hairs is present, and the tuft is not conspicuous, note the second glume which has an expanded base that tapers to the tip, it is *S. heterolepis* (prairie dropseed). Barrens, glades, prairies; UPL.

Sporobolus heterolepis

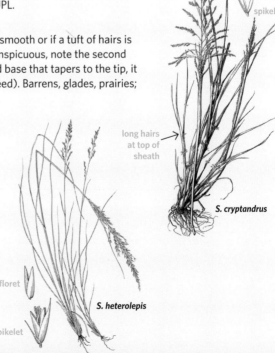

spikelet

long hairs at top of sheath

S. cryptandrus

floret

S. heterolepis

spikelet

If the lemmas are hairy (*S. vaginiflorus* is minutely hairy), go to

If the lemmas are smooth, not hairy, go to

If the inflorescence is 1–5 cm long and the seed is gelatinous when wet, it is *S. vaginiflorus* (poverty grass). Glades, barrens, open disturbed sites.

If the inflorescence is 5–11 cm long and the seed is loose but not gelatinous when wet, it is *S. clandestinus* (hidden dropseed). Glades, barrens, thin soils of woodlands.

Sporobolus vaginiflorus

Sporobolus clandestinus

S. vaginiflorus

flore

glume

S. clandestinus

If the glumes and lemma are ± equal in length, it is *S. neglectus* (puffsheath dropseed). Dry, rocky barrens and outcrops over calcareous rocks; UPL/FACU.

If the glumes and lemma are of three different lengths, go to

Sporobolus neglectus

floret

spikelet

S. neglectus

F

If the lemma is ≥ 3 mm long, and the first glume is ≥ 1.5 mm long, it is *S. compositus* [*S. asper*] (rough dropseed). Small grass of dry habitats. Calcareous glades and barrens, disturbed sites on calcareous rocks.

If the lemma is < 3 mm long, and the first glume is < 1.5 mm long, it is *S. indicus*† (smutgrass). Plants of wet, open soils. Roadsides, ditches.

Sporobolus compositus

Sporobolus indicus

floret

glumes

S. compositus

seed

spikelet

S. indicus

Urochloa [*Brachiaria*] (signalgrass, millet)

Urochloa platyphylla

Urochloa ramosa

U. platyphylla (broadleaf signalgrass). Upper part of the second glume and sterile lemma showing transverse veins, and spikelets 3.5-4.7 mm long. Impoundment shores, low roadsides, ditches.

U. ramosa (browntop millet). Upper part of the second glume and sterile lemma with obscure (or absent) transverse veins, and spikelets 2-4 mm long. Fields, waste ground.

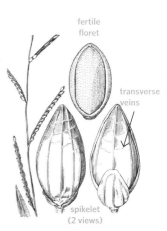

fertile floret

transverse veins

spikelet (2 views)

U. platyphylla

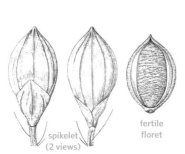

spikelet (2 views)

fertile floret

U. ramosa

Vulpia (fescue)

A If the first glume is ≤ one-half as long as the second, it is *V. myuros*† (foxtail fescue). Roadsides, fields, disturbed areas; FACU/UPL.

Vulpia myuros

If the first glume is > one-half as long as the second, go to **B**

glumes   florets

V. myuros

B If the lemmas are hairy, it is *V. sciurea* [*V. elliotea*] (squirrel-tail fescue). Sandy roadsides, fields, disturbed areas in the coastal plain.

If the lemmas are smooth or scabrous, go to **C**

Vulpia sciurea

V. sciurea   spikelet

C If the spikelets have five to eleven (or more) closely overlapping florets, and the awns of the lemmas are typically up to 9 mm long, it is *V. octoflora* (sixweeks fescue). Dry, sterile soils; FACU/UPL.

If the spikelets have four to seven loosely overlapping florets, and the awns of the lemmas are 3–12 mm long, it is *V. bromoides*† (brome fescue). Sandy, disturbed areas; UPL/FACW.

Vulpia octoflora

Vulpia bromoides

spikelet

V. octoflora

spikelet

V. bromoides

Zizania (wildrice)

Zizania palustris

Zizania aquatica

Z. aquatica (southern wildrice). ♀ lemmas thin, papery, dull, and minutely scabrous all over. Tidal and nontidal freshwater marshes; OBL.

Z. palustris (northern wildrice). ♀ lemmas firm, leathery, and scabrous along the veins and at the tip (where they taper into the awn), but otherwise shiny and smooth. Lakeshores; OBL.

♂ spikelet

♀ spikelet

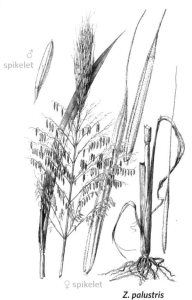

♂ spikelet

♀ spikelet

Z. palustris

Z. aquatica

References

Clayton, W. D., M. S. Vorontsova, K. T. Harman, and H. Williamson. 2006–. GrassBase—The Online World Grass Flora Descriptions. http://www.kew .org/data/grasses-db.html.

Gleason, H. A., and A. Cronquist. 1991. *Manual of Vascular Plants of the Northeastern United States and Adjacent Canada*. 2nd ed. Bronx, N.Y.: New York Botanical Garden.

Harmon, P. J., D. Ford-Werntz, and W. Grafton. 2006. *Checklist and Atlas of the Vascular Flora of West Virginia*. Elkins, W. Va.: West Virginia Division of Natural Resources, Wildlife Resources Section.

Hitchcock-Chase Collection of Grass Drawings. 2016. Hunt Institute for Botanical Documentation, Carnegie Mellon University, Pittsburgh, Pa. http://www.huntbotanical.org/databases/show.php?10.

Maryland Plant Atlas Work Group. 2016. Digital Atlas of the Maryland Flora. http:// http://www.marylandplantatlas.org/index.php.

McAvoy, W. A. 2017. The Flora of Delaware Online Database. Delaware Division of Fish and Wildlife, Species Conservation and Research Program, Smyrna, Del. http://www.wrc.udel.edu/de-flora/.

Omernik, J. M. 1987. "Ecoregions of the Conterminous United States." *Annals of the Association of American Geographers* 77 (1): 118–25.

Rhoads, A. F., and T. A. Block. 2007. *The Plants of Pennsylvania: An Illustrated Manual*. 2nd ed. Philadelphia: University of Pennsylvania Press.

The Pennsylvania Flora Project. 2017. Morris Arboretum of the University of Pennsylvania, Philadelphia, Pa. http://paflora.org/original/.

U.S. Army Corps of Engineers. 2016. National Wetland Plant List. Version 3.3. http://wetland_plants.usace.army.mil/.

U.S. Department of Agriculture / National Resources Conservation Service. PLANTS Database / A. S. Hitchcock (rev. A. Chase). *Manual of the Grasses of the United States*. USDA Miscellaneous Publication No. 200. Washington, D.C., 1950. http://plants.usda.gov.

Utah State University. Grass Manual on the Web. 2008. http://herbarium .usu.edu/webmanual/.

Verloove, F. 2016. *Manual of the Alien Plants of Belgium*. Botanic Garden of Meise, Belgium. http://alienplantsbelgium.be.

Virginia Botanical Associates. 2016. Digital Atlas of the Virginia Flora. Virginia Botanical Associates, Blacksburg, Va. http://www.vaplantatlas.org.

Weakley, A. S. 2015. "Flora of the Southern and Mid-Atlantic States." Working paper (as of May 21, 2015). http://www.herbarium.unc.edu /FloraArchives/WeakleyFlora_2015-05-29.pdf.

Weldy, T., D. Werier, and A. Nelson. 2017. New York Flora Atlas. New York Flora Association, Albany, N.Y. http://newyork.plantatlas.usf.edu/.

Plant Index

Index of scientific names

Index of common names

Numbers listed in **bold** indicate Genera Key page.

Photo Credits

The majority of the line drawings are from the Hitchcock-Chase Collection of Grass Drawings, on indefinite loan from the Smithsonian Institution, courtesy of the Hunt Institute for Botanical Documentation, Carnegie Mellon University, Pittsburgh, Pennsylvania.

Illustrations on pp. 2 (grass entry); 8 (leaf surface and ligule); 9, 21, and 27 (spike with two spikelets per node); 43 (boat-shaped leaf); 60 (clawlike auricle); and 145 (stem cross section) were drawn by the author.

Illustrations on pp. 5, 8, and 47 (open and closed sheaths); 9, 21, 27, and 73 (balanced and one-sided spikes, racemes, panicles, and digitate clusters); 13 (sessile and pedicellate spikelets); 21 (leaf with shiny midrib and leaf with wavy edges); 23 (split ligule); 25 (*S. bicolor* and spikelet); 31 and 73 (*E. villosa* and cuplike structure); 40 and 89 (*B. aristosum* and floret); 52 and 120 (auricle); 62 (hands); 105 (viscid ring); 106 (*D. scabriusculum* and mottled sheath); 107 (bearded node); 109 (papillose-hairy sheath); 115 (*E. wiegandii* and spikelet); 122 (*F. trachyphylla* and spikelet); and 152 (*S. bicolor* and spikelet pair) were drawn by Elizabeth Farnsworth. She has kindly granted permission for use of her images in this book.

Illustrations on pp. 86 (*A. aristatum* spikelet [side view]); 113 (*E. muricata* spikelets and floret); and 117 (leaf margin with glandular dots) are sourced from F. Verloove, *Manual of the Alien Plants of Belgium*, which can be accessed at http://alienplantsbelgium.be. Images are licensed under a Creative Commons CC BY-SA license, https://creativecommons.org/licenses/by-sa/2.0.

Illustrations on pp. 126 (*H. pusillum*); 156 (*S. clandestinus*); and 158 (*V. bromoides*) are from the USDA/NRCS PLANTS Database / A. S. Hitchcock (rev. A. Chase), *Manual of the Grasses of the United States*, USDA Miscellaneous Publication No. 200 (Washington, D.C., 1950), http://plants.usda.gov.

All maps were commissioned by the author.